"Dr Giazitzoglu provides a useful and practical guide for aspiring and current students in business schools. From more concrete issues such as finding a job, he provides a genuine account on how to make the most of the student experience."

—**Thomas Roulet**, *Professor of Organisational Sociology and Leadership at Judge Business School, University of Cambridge, UK.*

"*Studying Business at University: The Survival Guide* is an essential read for any student embarking on the business school journey. Drawing from a decade of experience, this book offers practical, down-to-earth advice on navigating the business school environment – from the first-year challenges to final-year projects. Written in an accessible and engaging style, the book is filled with rich detail which provokes the reader to reflect deeply on how students navigate a high-pressure atmosphere. What makes this [book] distinctive is its humour and real-world relevance. Giazitzoglu offers not just academic survival tips but advice for a diverse readership to thrive both inside and outside the classroom."

—**Garth Stahl**, *Associate Professor, University of Queensland, Australia.*

STUDYING BUSINESS AT UNIVERSITY

Taking a business degree at university – whether it is in management, marketing, operations management, finance, accounting, economics or another subject – is a fulfilling and rewarding experience. But how can you know, before you choose your subject, what it will be like? How is it possible to make an informed decision?

Look no further. *Studying Business at University* provides new and prospective undergraduates with a concise and easy-to-read insight into what life is like as a business student today. This student-friendly book, written in the style of an email dialogue between two students, informs and reassures the new business student who is seeking advice on how to get the most out of their degree experience and covers the whole degree from application to graduation – and beyond. Covering questions of employability, work placements, job interviews and emerging concerns such as the use of Artificial Intelligence (AI) in research and essays, this book is an up-to-date window on the modern student experience.

Ideal for final-year college students who are choosing their degree subject as well as undergraduates and international students who are actively navigating their way through their business degree course, this book will also be a helpful reference for lecturers who want to give their students as much support as possible as they learn to balance the demands of academia with the pressures of the real world.

Andreas Giazitzoglu is a Senior Lecturer and Associate Professor in the Sociology of Entrepreneurship and Organisations at Newcastle University Business School (UK).

STUDYING BUSINESS AT UNIVERSITY

The Survival Guide

Andreas Giazitzoglu

Routledge
Taylor & Francis Group

LONDON AND NEW YORK

Designed cover image: Tom Merton / OJO Images / Getty Images ®

First published 2025
by Routledge
4 Park Square, Milton Park, Abingdon, Oxon OX14 4RN

and by Routledge
605 Third Avenue, New York, NY 10158

Routledge is an imprint of the Taylor & Francis Group, an informa business

British Library Cataloguing-in-Publication Data
A catalogue record for this book is available from the British Library

Library of Congress Cataloging-in-Publication Data
Names: Giazitzoglu, Andreas, author.
Title: Studying business at university : the survival guide / Andreas Giazitzoglu.
Description: Abingdon, Oxon ; New York, NY : Routledge, 2025. | Includes index.
Identifiers: LCCN 2024046416 | ISBN 9781032740348 (hardback) | ISBN 9781032740423 (paperback) | ISBN 9781003467397 (ebook)
Subjects: LCSH: Business education. | Education, Higher. | Business schools.
Classification: LCC HF1106 .G53 2025 | DDC 650.071--dc23/eng/20250118
LC record available at https://lccn.loc.gov/2024046416

ISBN: 978-1-032-74034-8 (hbk)
ISBN: 978-1-032-74042-3 (pbk)
ISBN: 978-1-003-46739-7 (ebk)

DOI: 10.4324/9781003467397

Typeset in Times New Roman
by SPi Technologies India Pvt Ltd (Straive)

CONTENTS

ACKNOWLEDGEMENTS

For my girls (in order of appearance!): Emma, Heidi, Georgiana and Lydia.
For my Mam, my late Father and the late Grandma Joycie.
For the lads and lasses in my inner circle.
For Andrew Harrison at Routledge.
For all my amazing colleagues, in various sociology departments and business schools around the world.
A special shoutout for the *Flossmeister General*.
For friends at New Life and St Aldates, past and present.
For the kind and friendly baristas who made me lovely Double Espressos at Costa Coffee shop on Morpeth High Street (where I wrote most of this book).
For all Bus 1004ers, Bus 300ers, Bus 3343ers and NBS6824ers.
Most of all, for the Carpenter who saved my life.

INTRODUCTION

I wanted to write an epistolary book, depicting a series of letters between a student and a retired business school professor. The student would ask the professor key questions about what to expect at a business school and how to achieve at different points in the business school learning journey. It was my favourite author of all time – CS Lewis – who gave me the idea to use an epistolary format to explore how to survive a business school.

Lewis used an epistolary format in his brilliant *The Screwtape Letters*, though his letters contain correspondence between demonic forces. Thankfully, the characters of these letters are more benevolent! I found a superb editor at Routledge – Andrew Harrison – who encouraged me to develop the idea into a book. Andrew also pointed out that letters are pretty much obsolete and that the professor I envisaged sounded like the one from *The Lion, Witch and the Wardrobe!* What an anachronism I had become. So, we decided to write a book based on emails *not* letters, with the concept of 'surviving' business school underpinning the e-mails and the e-mails collectively representing a survival guide. Instead of a kindly professor advising a student, I thought a student could e-mail two other students, with more experience, to get advice.

I wrote the book as a Senior Lecturer, with over 10 years of experience at Newcastle University Business School. (That's the Newcastle in the Northeast of England, not Australia). By the point of writing this book, I had lectured thousands of students, supervised hundreds of dissertations and supervised 5 PhDs to completion. I came to work in a business school largely by accident. I trained as a qualitative researcher in Anthropology and Sociology. I was on the dole and walked into the Newcastle University Business School one day, partly out of boredom, partly out of intrigue and mainly because my girlfriend

DOI: 10.4324/9781003467397-1

(now wife) parked in front of it, and the building seemed intriguing and miles away from the sociology and anthropology buildings at Durham and Oxford, where I'd studied.

By chance, a colleague at Newcastle University Business School – whom I met serendipitously – needed a Research Associate to design qualitative methods. I got the chance to design some research methods, seeing the link between entrepreneurship and social science for the first time and I loved it. I ended up staying, reinventing myself as a business school scholar (to the surprise of sociologists I know and the bewilderment of some business scholars I know). I realised there was an interesting intersection between sociology and business, that I could teach and research.

Why this matters? It matters because I came to a business school as an outsider, and had to learn the rules of the place to survive. I had no survival guide. All these years on, thinking about students, it struck me that there isn't really a 'survival guide' book for them; a book for business school students to consult. I thought I might be able to write a book that would help students, based on my own experiences of engaging with students daily. I also remember reading *Letters to a Law Student*, when I had seriously considered reading law as a student and wanted to provide a framework akin to that in *Letters to a Law Student* that has utility and relevance to business school students, by which I mean a framework that business school students could dip into and consult to get answers on specific aspects of their learning journey. From these roots, this book emerged.

I have mainly engaged with marketing, management and entrepreneurship students. I wrote for them, to help future students studying these disciplines. I did so as these are the subjects that most, though not all, of the students I have taught studied. But I feel that much of what I write will apply to students studying other subjects in business school, and other subjects in a university more generally. I hope this is the case. The book is written primarily for the British undergraduate business school context. But much of the work is transferable and applicable to business schools in other national contexts and – certainly – students coming into business schools for taught master's degrees. I hope the book is especially relevant to students who have come to the UK from other national contexts and are currently studying, and who will find direction and answers in the book within a system that can be bewildering.

Initially, I wrote the book to depict e-mails between two characters: Adam and Eve. Eve is in the year above Adam – a year older and considerably wiser. So, Eve can answer Adam's questions with a sense of 'been there done that' experience. But I added a third character – Titus. This was to diversify the answers that Adam received to his questions. In case anyone is reading this and thinking 'are Adam, Eve and Titus real'?, the answer is no. They are fictitious. Or more accurately, they are 'types': somewhat stereotypical, even marginally cliched, versions of students I've met over the years. They ask and respond to questions in ways that I'd expect – based on experience – types of students to do.

Eve is like so many (though not all!) of my students at Newcastle: bright, kind, ambitious and thoughtful. A high achieving Russell group student who gets a first and ends up with job offers. She provides the 'right' answers to Adam's questions, or at least the answers that I and my colleagues think are right and would like students to hear and, even better, act upon. Adam is a little unsure about whether to go to business school. He then spends most of his first year self-sabotaging before pulling his socks up after almost failing his first year. He gets through his three years and ends up with a 2:1. He has options. He does well to listen to Eve.

Titus is at a campus-based university. He is a perceptive commentator on university life – and life in general. Titus' e-mails provide a narrative that is distinct from Eve's. Titus gives answers to Adam's questions that are rooted in lifestyle choices and broader life experiences. Eve is all about detail, breaking down the academic side of surviving business school and writing very much in the now. Adam looks outside of the university. He enjoys university life as it's so different to 'the old town': the place he lived before studying at university, which he finds suffocating and wishes to escape from. Titus – like Eve – is a year older than Adam, though Adam and Titus end up in the same stage of their degrees (though at different universities) because Titus spends a year in industry between his second and final years. Titus excels in the workplace.

Writing from the perspective of Adam allows me to give 'survival' lessons that apply to life outside of studying. In contrast, Eve's focus is very much on directing how best to achieve academically. Through Titus, I was able to offer advice that is at times bordering on the philosophical and – in my view at least – humorous. In juxtaposition, Eve's e-mails are erudite. But the primary point is that by inventing these characters and their correspondence, real students can learn real information about how to survive and achieve at a business school. Some may prefer Titus, some may prefer Adam. The point is to learn what you need from them.

Within the e-mail correspondence, I have referred to a number of books that I hope readers of this survival guide will locate and engage with. These books say a lot more than I can! Part of the survival guide is consulting the works of others to help survive better and in more specialised ways. But if students don't know which 'others' to go to, the existence of such books is somewhat irrelevant. In this context, I've referred to books that are not 'traditionally' academic. I've done this as I wanted to select books that I think students will actually enjoy and learn from, and which contain narratives and perspectives that may seem – refreshingly – different to what they've read so far.

I have to be honest: I feel sorry for some young people today. Contemporary versions of Titus, Eve and their peers – through no fault of their own – have been conditioned in a system that has not really done them many favours academically, at least in terms of encouraging them to think for themselves and hear voices outside of a narrow – very 'safe' – stream. (They've also not been shown how to write, but that's a different gripe). When I suggest a book, I do so in the hope of broadening students' minds and allowing others to help do what universities are meant to do (but are perhaps finding it harder to do these days). Namely prepare students for the world out there – as it is, rather than how some ivory tower academic or HR professional might wish it was. It's a world in which students must find work, make ends meet, deal with stress and – in my view – compete, achieve, succeed and find fulfilment. And also have fun. Don't forget to have fun! The books I suggest might help with these rather grandiose, aims.

This book is structured over six chapters, with each chapter trying to help students at distinctive points in their business school experience or 'learning journey'. Readers can read it all in one chunk or 'dip in' to chapters as they need to, depending on where they are in their degree. I'll summarise each chapter, below.

Chapter 1 is written for students thinking about applying to business schools (so students doing A levels or other pre-university qualifications and who are close to completing UCAS forms and other university application forms). The chapter is also written for students who have offers from business schools, who have not yet started studying for their degrees and who want an insight into what is coming. If students are tentative or unsure about going to a business school, having already got an offer, I hope this chapter will be useful to them as they make a decision that has life-changing ramifications. I want to encourage people to come to business school! But I also want to point out that there are other options – university is not for everyone and not for everyone right now! The chapter is also written for students who, in their first few weeks or semester of business school, are a little bewildered about where they are and what they are meant to be doing. Chapter 1 contains an e-mail exchange between Adam (at this point applying to business schools) and Eve (at this point in her first year studying at a business school). Eve discusses what she has learned and experienced so far, highlighting in particular how university is different to school and why these differences matter in terms of adapting. Chapter 1 also consists of an e-mail exchange between Adam and Titus. Titus is also in his first year at this point. Titus discusses university life (as distinct from business school life) more broadly. He points out the sorts of societies he has encountered and some of the characters that populate them.

Chapter 2 helps students get to grips with the basics of university life, which will not seem so basic when they have to be learned quickly in the first few weeks of being at a business school. Chapter 2 consists of an e-mail exchange between Adam – in his first few weeks – and Eve, who is now in her second year and academically thriving. Eve explains grade categories, time management, assessments, lectures and seminars. These are the foundations of university life! Chapter 2 also has an e-mail exchange between Adam and Titus. Titus – also now in his second year – describes a series of lessons to Adam. Titus learned these lessons after a summer of learning. The lessons are practical and aim to help readers live a life that gives them the best chance of achieving all they might by cultivating a healthy mind, body and lifestyle. Several books are discussed by Titus, which I hope readers will go on to locate and read. I hope the chapter doesn't sound preachy. If you manage to implement all the rules, you might be the most-rounded student in the UK!

Chapter 3 takes place in semester 2 of Adam's first year, just as Adam is about to complete his most important set of university assessments to date. I wrote this chapter in the hope that readers will return to this chapter when they approach key assessment times, in years one, two, three and later (e.g. if they are post-graduate students). The context of Chapter 3 is that Adam is stressed, unprepared and in danger of failing the first year. Eve gives clarity, explaining what to do, the different modes of assessment Adam faces and puts the first year into context. How description and analysis differ and why this difference matters in terms of getting good grades is made clear, as are the foundations of making logical arguments. It is these dimensions of Eve's e-mail that I think students should revisit as their learning journey evolves. Assessments are perhaps the most important part of a business school – they will determine how a student does in terms of grades. So, I wanted to explain how I think you can do well in assessments. Chapter 3 also contains a forthright, direct e-mail from Titus, suggesting Adam grows up and 'disappears' to focus on work and maximise his chances of passing the year. Titus again considers the importance of rules and how certain rules can be applied to and help in Adam's situation.

Chapter 4 takes place in Adam's second year. Adam passed his first year, despite the challenges that came his way at the end of year one. At this point in his journey, Adam has found a new level of enthusiasm for his degree. He is more settled with the academic dimensions of university life (aided by Eve's advice) and now has questions about employability. Chapter 4 sees an e-mail response between Adam and Eve. Eve is now in her third and final year. She is sanguine about Adam getting a job while studying. Eve has a number of job offers, following a rigorous application process, which she discusses. Chapter 4 also contains two e-mail exchanges between Adam and Titus. Titus is now doing a placement year. Titus has found work at a local management consultancy firm. The firm is a good 'fit' for him. In the first e-mail, written in semester 1, Titus discusses his early experiences of working in this firm. In a later e-mail, written in late summer before Adam and Titus start their third and final year of study, Titus discusses in further detail his experiences of working in industry for a year. He talks about the people and processes he encountered. These emails are about surviving work, as much as about surviving business school. They position work as an integral part of the business school experience and, therefore, as an integral part of surviving business school.

Chapter 5 sees Adam contact Eve again. Eve, now in the world of work, discusses more about what to do in the final and third year of study. Eve details the dissertation process. She also gives advice on how to deal with large amounts of reading and how to use what you read in ways that help substantiate assignments. Though written in the context of Adam's final year, the 'survival' discussions here are also useful to students writing assessments in their other years and complement the assignment-focused discussions that occur earlier, in Chapter 3.

Chapter 6 sees Adam reflect on his time at university. He contemplates what options he now has, having passed his degree. He realises he enjoyed studying, and wishes he'd taken advantage of all the opportunities he had, while a student. He is pleasantly surprised by how some of his course-mates with borderline grades were treated via the 'board of examiners' process. Unlike Eve, Adam does not have a job to start after graduation. His future is uncertain, as it is for most students at this point in their learning journey. He has options – such as travelling, further study and getting a job. These options are discussed.

The book ends with an epilogue, in which the sorts of futures that students like Adam, Eve and Titus might experience are discussed. It projects how things are about five years after Adam's final e-mail.

Andreas Giazitzoglu.
Stannington, Morpeth, Northumberland. 2024.

1

AN INTRODUCTION TO BUSINESS SCHOOL

Part One: Will Business School be Right for Me?

Adam is 17 years old and is in his final year of school education. He is interested in studying a business degree at university but is not sure whether university is the right choice for him. Adam's mum is friends with the mum of a girl from the year above Adam at school – Eve – who is currently in her first semester at university, on a business degree. Adam's mum encourages him to email Eve to ask her what studying business at university is really like, and after some initial procrastination, he does…

SUBJECT: APPLYING TO BUSINESS SCHOOL?

From: Adam
To: Eve
Date: Around when the UCAS form/university application is due

Hi Eve,
You're probably wondering why I'm sending this email. Basically, my Mum says you're now at a business school. I'm thinking of applying to study business at university myself and have a few questions I love to ask you if that's okay.

1. Can you tell me what business school is like?
2. How did you decide to study business?
3. How did you choose a specific business school to study at?

DOI: 10.4324/9781003467397-2

I want to get a sense of whether business school is right for me before I get into debt and spend years of my life studying at one. I see you as someone 'on the inside' and myself as 'on the outside'. Any inside information is welcome, so I can make a decision that is more informed. Neither of my parents went to university so I don't know who else to ask.

Thanks a lot!
Adam

The following day, Adam receives a reply.

Subject: RE: Applying to Business School?

From: Eve
To: Adam

Dear Adam,
It's nice to hear from you. Thanks for your email! It's true, I am at a business school. 😌
    Last year, when I was thinking about going to university, I remember feeling as you seem to now: excited but nervous and with questions. It's normal, I suppose. And it's definitely best to get answers to the questions you're asking. Though remember, everyone will have different answers, and, in the end, you must make a choice that is best for you. But an informed choice is better than an optimistic 'I hope it'll all be okay' approach. And an informed choice is certainly better than a 'because it's out of my comfort zone and unfamiliar I'll avoid it' mentality. I am on the inside, as you describe it. So, I'll try my best to help.
    This time last year I was going to different open days, visiting business schools and trying to project myself into the future, thinking how things might be if I started studying and where to go to study. I'm not sure it was all that healthy, looking back: it's best to deal with the now, which is where you are, rather than the future, which you have no real knowledge of. What that means for you right now is doing well in your A levels, getting the applications in and deciding where you want to go, with that decision being based on logic and common sense, as much as it can be. Business schools looked so polished and promising when I visited during open days. During open days, they handed out lovely free bags and pens. Happy, charming existing students showed us around while emphasising why this particular business school I'm visiting is the best.

(Coincidentally, if you get the chance to go to some open days, I suggest you go!). But these open days are designed to give you an insight into the best aspects of the business school. They are maybe reflections of how things should be, rather than how things are.

I always knew I wanted to go to a business school. I always knew I wanted to go to university. There was nothing else that interested me. Maybe I'd been conditioned to think this. Maybe I lacked options and imagination. Or maybe the path well-trodden is well trodden for a reason: it works and has worked, so it's replicated. So, in a sense, my decision was easier than it might have been if I was not totally sure or committed to the idea of being a business school student one day. I was at an advantage over someone like you, who doesn't know, with certainty, what they want to do. More accurately, I was interested in management and marketing as specific aspects of business. I wanted to study and learn about these areas. That is the degree I am on now: a three-year degree with learning ('modules') split roughly in half, between those taught and focused on management, and the others on marketing. But you can study lots of subjects in business schools: accountancy, economics, entrepreneurship, business studies, international business and strategy. All sorts. That's not an exhaustive list. And business schools offer courses all the way from undergraduate degrees – the sort I am studying now and you will apply to out of sixth form – to doctorates and MBAs. I think what I say below applies to most if not all subjects you might study at a business school; though probably less to 'mathematical' subjects like accountancy and economics, which are their own sort of subcultures in business schools with quite unique disciplinary rules and norms.

Think of business schools as big buildings on university campuses that tend to host lots of students (especially international students) studying various topics. They are busy, fast places. But they are fun. They are often new buildings architecturally which can be impressive. They are the 'growth' areas of modern universities. They often fund other departments, at a time when other departments are struggling to recruit students. One thing I've noticed is that you meet loads of people, whether you want to or not. Networking is a big part of life and a feature of business school, and university more broadly. Business schools – and I speak plurally here because this is true for my business school and those my friends attend – will go out of their way to integrate students and form a sense of community and collective among the cohorts, right from the first day you start. (Or at least business schools that care about their students will do this). That said, the onus is on you as an individual to take advantage of these opportunities and make new friends, within the structures the business school provides. You'll not like everyone you meet, of course. You'll certainly meet people from backgrounds different to yours and who express views different to yours. This is a great thing, even if it might cause you to feel out of your comfort zone to start with. After all, the world is a diverse place, full of different sorts of people and various opinions. It's good to get used to mixing with different types of people, from different places and backgrounds, and learning from them. Indeed, that is one of the most important things you'll learn at a university.

Hope this helps!
Eve

Hi Eve,
Thanks so much for getting back to me.

It's kind of scary that at 17 I have to make a decision that will impact the rest of my life. If you go to medical school, that's it, you're a medical doctor. If you go to dentistry school, that's it, you're a dentist. If you go to ... well, you see where I'm going with this. I'm thinking about going to business school. That's partly because I don't really know what else I want to do and partly because business seems kind of interesting and relevant as something to study and – more importantly – as something that will give me options after I graduate. After all, there's no point in spending time and money, and lots of time and money, doing something at university with limited prospects in the end. I don't want to spend years of my life and thousands of pounds studying something as if it's a hobby, rather than studying something that will give me skills and experiences that will 'count' out there, in the real world, where there are bills to pay. While I'm studying, I'm not just incurring debt, I'm also giving up on getting money and experience in a job – even the sort of job others might look down on and sneer at. The point is this is a defining time in my life, and the decision I make is a big one. It'll have implications that are ongoing.

I'm in sixth form now. I'm at the point when I need to start applying to universities and tailoring my personal statement to 'fit' with the degrees I apply to.

Anyway, I best get back to schoolwork and let you get back to business school – whatever that means.

Thanks, Adam.

Hi Adam,

You're right, there probably is more of a focus on employment and employability in business schools than there is in other departments in terms of what they teach and what they aim to do to you as a learner (or 'customer', if you want to be cynical). For example, I know people in History, Classics and English departments. They love their subjects but don't seem to have a clear career track. What will they actually do at the end of their degrees (other than teach)? This isn't necessarily a problem. Why should someone know what they want? That said, I like to have a sense of direction. A target to aim for. I can see how I have options to do work experience as part of my degree (a year in industry) and also how the cases and theories we are taught by our lecturers can be transferred into the world of work. The better lecturers will say things like 'if they ask you in a job interview about x, then you might talk about case y to answer' or 'when you're working, it will probably make sense to implement these principles and strategies because it worked for x under these circumstances so is worth considering again in a contemporary context'. I guess they're priming us for the world of work which, my lecturers have emphasised, is incredibly cut-throat and competitive. So, behind the shiny buildings, business schools should have an employment focus.

That said, my degree is not 'vocational' or 'training'. It's higher education – which means theories and learning and writing and reading – but education with a purpose. I think this is something a lot of students get confused about. You might hear phrases like 'theory meets practice' to sum up what business schools are doing. They teach you cases or 'case studies', to see how business has occurred and manifested in the past. They analyse the cases, so you can learn the importance of them and the wider lessons from them. But they don't then give you a business, for you to replicate the case as a sort of project or plaything! (Though you can start a business in your own time). On top of this learning, things are put in place so you can go out and tell the world what you know and, therefore, tell people in the world why they should employ you, so that you can help them manage their people or market their products. We even get employers coming to our business school to recruit us.

There are employability weeks at my business school and the business schools my friends are at. In these weeks, you meet recruiters, work on CVs and practice interview skills. All sorts. But my course is not a 'how to' course. As I said before and emphasise here, it's not vocational training and nor should it, even can it, be. As one of my lecturers said, if I could tell you exactly how to grow a business and make millions through simple steps that always work everywhere, I wouldn't be here teaching – I'd be on a boat, in the sun, drinking cocktails. What's it for, then? What is the reason for coming here? I guess it's partly so that you can get a piece of paper (a degree) that people 'out there' recognise and which tells them: this person has studied, they have a certain amount of knowledge, they have certain skills and therefore you might want to take a close look at them, as potential employees. People out there themselves may have the same piece of paper. Ideally, the piece of paper will have value and currency all over the world. In that sense, it's a passport. It's a way to demonstrate and symbolise what you can contribute.

It's worth pointing out that there are lots of different business schools, just like there are lots of different universities. Most universities have a business school attached to them. Geography and place are important to someone like you, selecting which business school they might apply to and end up at. Why spend three or four years in a place you don't like, or a place where you don't feel like you fit in or which doesn't offer the things you want outside of your degree? Of course, you can find universities in big cities or small cities and towns. So, where you study, or apply to study, in terms of place is really a personal choice, and probably linked to how far away from home you want to be (or not) and whether you really like a place and want to be there, and whether you want a big city or a smaller campus or collegiate feel. Coincidently, don't rule out living at home and attending a local business school – there are advantages to this, especially saving on rent and perhaps tapping into local networks to get employment opportunities during and after your degree! But for me, I wanted to fly the nest, live in a new place and meet new people. So staying at home wasn't the right option for me as an individual. Also, this particular business school where I study is extremely well regarded for marketing. It is recognised as producing very employable marketing graduates. So that was a pull for me.

Generally speaking, most cities will have a 'posh v poly' dynamic at play. If this sounds weird it is because it is, intrinsically, weird and, in my view, snobby. What it is getting at is that in cities there is normally an older, more established 'red brick' university and a newer university, which was probably a polytechnic before a lot of former polytechnics became universities in the 1990s. There is typically rivalry between these universities. This rivalry is expressed in sports, primarily. But the rivalry is normally good natured. Having a posh and a poly in most cities means that you have a decent chance of ending up in the geographical place you want to study, as if your grades aren't high enough for a 'posh' university, then they might be for a former poly. Newer universities might attract a more local student body.

But don't think the old versus new university status is a sign of quality, per se. Lots of new universities are outperforming older ones now, in various ways. (Compare student satisfaction rates, employment rates etc. between institutions).

Don't assume an older, grander university is 'better' in general or for you as a person. You must ask what sort of university environment you need and try and access a university that can provide that. Because the older universities tend to be more research focused, you might find the academics at older universities more focused on publishing their research than teaching. This might not matter for highly motivated students who can read a lot outside of their lectures. But for other students, they will require academics who are teachers first, and researchers second (if at all) to support them. So what is best for you? And which university is able to deliver that? These are vital questions for you to consider, in mind of the choice and variation out there.

It's possible – and ironic – that you will be taught at a business school by someone who has never actually done any business in their lives! Only studied it. I've been taught several aspects of business (including 'leadership', 'management' and 'start-up') by people who have never 'done business'; people who went to university and stayed there, becoming academics and who are now teaching, and often teaching badly. It might be that when choosing a university, you want a mix of lecturers with academic backgrounds (who will probably publish research articles – more on those below) – and people who came to university having worked in the industry. One friend of mine is being taught how to run a business by lecturers who have never themselves run a business! How much can they really know outside of the 'ivory tower' view of business? The lecturers seem oblivious to their own shortcomings and lack of knowledge as they talk about their research – often with pride and hubris – into what seems a really obscure aspect of business which can leave one feeling 'but what does this mean for me?' I know I'm meant to be involved in some sort of worship here because you wrote this article, but stepping back from the expectation, how does this help me now? However, the newer universities may have people teaching you who have 'done the business' so to speak, rather than just trying to theorise about business. Does this sound like something that is important to you as an individual, even if it means the buildings you study in are newer and the reputation of the university may seem less elite? Or is being in a university culture where research is the main priority really important to you? At the end of the day, you're a 'paying customer', to put it bluntly. And you can expect bang for your buck. What place has the structure in place that is best for this to happen to you, as an individual?

Linked to this: Russell Group business schools. I found out after I came to university that there are a group of universities called Russell Groups, and they tend to be the most prestigious. In other words, these are the 'posh', older universities discussed above, with quads, gardens and red brick buildings. As I said, I hear that Russell Group Universities are more 'research focused' and 'academic', while other, newer universities are more teaching focused. It's worth thinking about your learning style and what suits you and the sort of job you want after you graduate. If you want to work at a big posh city firm – one of those elite, multinational organisations with lucrative pay and long hours – you should know that such firms look more favourably on a Russell Group degree. They might assume there is a level of rigour with a Russell Group degree. Those recruiting probably went to a Russell Group university themselves. But at the end of the day, people will employ you for who you are.

Universities are ranked. There are specific rankings for business schools, and these seem to be a big deal. In fact, I know friends at other business schools, where those business schools are obsessed with how they appear in rankings. They spend so long trying to 'game the system' (i.e. to get students to say good things about the business school in surveys) that they forget about actually teaching the students! That's an exaggeration, of course, but you get the point. There are even international rankings! British universities do well, but the powerhouse reputations that British universities once enjoyed are perhaps not what it was. It's worth looking at where the top schools are for your subjects when applying. I mentioned before that the Russell Group business school I study at is a top place for marketing. They know it, the market knows it, the rankings 'prove it' and those applying to it are aware of it. Though how much onus to put on rankings? It's not for me to say. Another thing I learned – especially when I was going to business school open days – is to do with accreditation. Business schools have to go through all sorts of processes to get accreditations, which are meant to prove their prestige, status and value to you as a learner. The best business schools are said to be 'triple accredited'. Again, this is something to perhaps take into account when thinking about which business schools to apply to. Only 1% of the world's business schools are triple accredited. A large amount of these are based in the UK! It's good to mention on your CV that the university you went to is part of this elite group.

Got to run now but do message me if you think of anything else you want to ask me.

Eve

Thanks Eve. I'd never thought about business schools in those terms before. What would you say the main pros and cons of being at a business school are, from your perspective?

Adam

Hey Adam,

I'm only in my first year, but already it seems that there are many pros to being at business school. The first is the diversity of what you study and learn. You learn information from lecturers who lecture to you and seminars, which are like mini lectures. You also read in between lecturers. There really is so much information to take in. The best lecturers enable you to see the world – not just the world of business – in new ways. They give fresh perspectives. They challenge you to think and challenge you to think about why you think what you think. This may seem odd to start. Aren't they meant to affirm us and encourage us, rather than challenge us? The answer is unequivocally no! My degree is well structured. We study modules, with each module making up the year's syllabus. Our modules are taught over two semesters, with Christmas in between semesters one and two. Each module is assessed. There are exams, essays and presentations at the level of assessment, so you are judged – that is assessed or examined – through different methods. We only need to get 40% to pass this – the first – year. We are told often that what we are learning here in the first year are the skills we need for years two and three when our grades count towards our degree. A couple of my more candid lecturers have said they need to spend the first year knocking all the bad habits and lazy thinking school taught us, which I found funny. Judging from what my friends at other business schools have told me, the outline for the first year I described above is typical for most, maybe all, first-year business school students: a number of modules taught through lectures and seminars with assessments at the end of both semesters.

These pros also create cons. So much information? That can be overwhelming, especially when trying to use what we've been taught in assessments; when that information has to be engaged with in relation to a set task (like used to inform an essay). But engaging with information is a skill the lecturers are trying to teach us. Specifically, they seem to be cultivating the skill of evaluating lots of information and choosing specific information to form arguments and answers and address problems. They like detailed narrow answers and focus in essays here at the business school ('say everything about some *thing*, not something about everything' as one lecturer says). They want some original thought at university, in a way school didn't ask for when it seemed to be more 'rote' and more about memorising and repeating information and telling people (teachers) things they already believe to be true. Here, at business school it seems to be more about evaluating and working with information and coming to your own view, thereby evidencing viewpoints through analysis and data and facts; recognising subjectivities and nuance; and acknowledging that 'truth' is elusive.

There's also a shift to independent learning at university, which I, and many friends, have probably found the most different thing to school. I am adjusting to this transition. They are trying to help us transition from – as one lecturer said – 'spoon fed' students to students who can 'go away and read and learn on your own'. In this sense, a lecturer is very different to a teacher. Lecturers teach; but their teaching is more of a guiding process, showing students the different views and theories and then where to go to read and learn more about these. I seem to spend a lot of time reading, following up on the suggested reading my lecturers recommend. There was a sense of isolation and alienation for me to start with, as I sat for hours reading journal articles and books and trying to figure out which elements of what I'm reading are important. But, at the same time, I encountered a sense of intellectual autonomy and freedom and discovery. It is in assignments where we evidence that we have understood what we have been told to read and where we bring our learning together into a cohesive answer and response.

One key thing I'd recommend to you if you do end up at a business school: get to know your journals! By this I mean the journals where your lecturers publish work and which they say you should read. These journals host peer-reviewed research. So, your lecturers would have done their own research and then presented their research in an article; they then send that article to a journal and after a complex process of review, that research is published. Journals contain several articles that have gone through this process. Journals are the only way to keep up to date with the latest research, findings and arguments in your field. Time reading key journal articles is invaluable. Though the language of these articles and their complexity seemed to me and my course-mates quite intimidating at the start. That said, the more you learn by reading articles, the easier it will be to write about areas in an informed, confident way. A good hint – journal articles will give an overview of an area, showing what has been written to date and why it matters (and also research gaps). Find an article that summarises the area you're trying to understand. You'll be amazed at how much context and background knowledge a clearly written 'review' article will give you! Best of all, you'll be amazed how your marks will rocket when you demonstrate to lecturers that you know what the field is 'about' and what perspectives, polemics, innovations and contestations make up the field.

Eve

Hi Eve,

Thanks again. This is all quite overwhelming, to be honest. It seems like university will be kind of like school, but with a lot more boxes to tick! All the research, the journals and the lectures and seminars. It sounds pretty intimidating to be honest. I do wonder whether I'll be happy doing all that for three whole years. Maybe it would be easier to decide if my own parents had been to uni.

Adam

Hi Adam,

Well, there are options other than business school; in fact, options other than university. Some parents went to university and all their friends went to university and their friends' children are expected to go. So, these parents want and expect their kids to go. The motivation is probably well intentioned. But the pressure can be suffocating. University is not necessarily right for the child in question, but exploring alternative options is not allowed. You can imagine what typically happens to students at university when they don't want to be there but feel pressured to stay there. Some parents didn't go to university but really want their children to go despite having no sense of what a university is for or what it will do; these parents may idealise the university experience and impose unrealistic expectations. Again, the motivation on the part of the parents is benevolent, but the expectations set will be myopic. Another sort of parent will try and dissuade their child from going to university. Perhaps, they are scared that they will 'lose' their child in some way – geographically and culturally. In less benevolent cases, perhaps they resent their child being successful and feel intimidated by the prospect of their child 'bettering' them, even if just subconsciously.

The truth is university is not for everyone. But it is for some, indeed for quite a lot! Parents can and will influence. But pleasing your parents is not the aim if pleasing them doesn't please you. So, it's worth knowing that there are options and you're not bound to go to university. There are other, viable choices, and some of these choices have their own advantages. You could learn a trade. It's hard work. And it's perhaps not the option some families will encourage their children to take. But a trade – like being a plumber or electrician – means steady work for life, and you will start earning earlier and you won't incur masses of debt.

I felt huge pressure from school, family and friends to go to university. I know others felt this pressure. Some went to university as they felt obliged to go and didn't know what else to do. They didn't want to disappoint others. This is well meaning. But it's a terrible long-term strategy for them and their mental health and well-being. They don't really love the subject they're studying. They seem disengaged and frustrated. This is inevitable. Perhaps they should have got a trade? Why not follow your own path, even if that means not going to university, or delaying university enrolment until later in your life, when you might be more mature and more convinced university is the right path?

Other options aren't emphasised. Personally, I am glad I came to university. I am excited to see how the degree plays out and I feel optimistic about the future I might have, which my degree will play a part in. I want a 'graduate' job. It's hard to get one without a degree. I also want an education qualification that will be recognised all over the world and not be too specific to one place. For me then, this was the right choice. I will leave with debt. That will have to be paid. That is not ideal, to put it kindly. But I feel confident that the debt is worth it and that I will pay it off. That said, I feel obliged to point out that university is not for everyone. But let's put it this way: look into the statistics. University in general and business schools in particular are worth the investment of time and money you will put in, in terms of future earnings, if you want to reduce the experience to this measurement. So, at a pecuniary level, it is a good idea! You will earn more (or statistically are likely to earn more) over the course of a working lifetime with a good degree. Is that because of the degree or the individual? In other words, is this success because of what the degree teaches or because of the sort of people who do degrees? An interesting philosophical question but not one that really matters if you realise a degree gives you opportunities, that you can then take advantage of.

There isn't a right or wrong answer for you, then, to the question of if you should apply and – assuming you get the offer and grades – enrol at a business school. Likewise, there is not a simple answer about where to study or what to study. These are personal choices unique to you. It is perhaps intimidating to accept this. But the agency and choice are also exciting. I can't tell you what to do. But I hope the advice above will help YOU, as an individual, make your choice in a more informed way. And remember, if you decide against higher education now, it doesn't mean you can't revisit the idea in the future.

I am looking forward to hearing what you decide to do, and I will try and answer any further questions you have in the future, as an 'insider'.

Good luck!
Eve

Part Two: A Second Opinion

Adam feels like he's learned a lot from Eve's advice but thinks there's no harm in getting a second opinion. He writes to Titus, an old friend who is studying business at a different university from Eve.

SUBJECT: APPLYING TO BUSINESS SCHOOL?

From: Adam
To: Titus

Hi Titus,
Adam here. I used to play rugby for the same team as you. I miss playing rugby with you. We have had an ok season, but we missed you and some of the other lads who left to go to uni. Anyway, I remember you went to study at a business school. I am thinking of applying to one. I am doing my A levels now. What do you reckon? What's university like? I sent my friend, Eve, an email asking her what business school is like – as she is also studying at one. I got a good reply from her, but thought I'd ask you your views, too. I'm especially interested in the sorts of people you've come across.

Hope to hear from you soon.
All the best,
Adam

Subject: Applying to Business School?

From: Titus
To: Adam

Hello Adam. It's lovely to hear from you. I have good memories of you. Yeah, I left the old town and the old rugby club and came to university. I am at a business school, studying management. So, you heard correctly, and I can certainly try and help answer your questions. I was desperate to get away from the life I was living. I found the place suffocating and parochial. I wanted to live in a new place. I wanted to put distance between myself and others who were in my life. But I didn't want to go somewhere that was too big and where I'd be lost and overwhelmed. It was clear that certain universities in massive cities would have overwhelmed me and made me feel alienated. I like close-knit communities, small places and routines. I like being recognised. So, I came to a small business school which is part of a campus-based university. I love the place. I have made some really nice friends. I chose management as I want to manage people one day and believe I have some good leadership skills that I want to build on and enhance through my degree. I believe some people are born leaders and I think I might be one! But I also believe aspects of leadership – in terms of how to communicate and how to understand others – have to be learned and refined. That's why I came here, that's what motivated me.

I actually missed the grades required to study here. But on results day, I called up and spoke to the admissions tutor and they still let me in. Others I met here came through 'clearing'. So the lesson? On results day, if things aren't what you want, don't despair. There could be room for negotiation. If you really want to go to a business school but, for whatever reason, don't have the grades, don't give up. Well-rounded admission tutors realise there are more ways to assess the suitability and aptitude of a potential student than on exam grades alone!

You've asked me about business school specifically. One thing I can say is that business school is very different to school; or certainly different to the sort of school we attended. If you want to continue your experiences of school, then I don't think a degree is the best path for you. Perhaps, stay in the old town with others who have stayed there. There is comfort and security in that. Find a job. Don't think about what could have been. Let's start with how a degree is structured, as a 'program' or 'pathway'. The degree is made up of different modules. In year one, all of the modules we study are set for us by the business school. In years two and three, we will study some 'core' modules (which you have to study, and which are set) and also 'optional' ones, so you can choose topics that are more interesting and relevant to you. This is the case at most business schools.

I go to lectures for each module. These tend to happen the same day each week. You get in a rhythm. I find the early morning lectures hard to attend as I don't like mornings, especially if I was out the night before. Lectures can be dull – you just sit there listening – though a couple of the modules are really engaging, and the lectures for these modules are well attended. It's interesting to see where types of students sit in the lecture. Even though I am at a relatively small business school, there are still around 100 other students in the lecture. In the front rows, the very motivated students sit. They take notes. They are engaged. They always attend. They will even answer questions if asked. At the back and in the middle, you get other sorts of students. Some listen, some listen some of the time and some just spend the lecture on their phone or pretending to take notes on an expensive, gleaming laptop while really playing games or scrolling social media. I think some students just attend to try and find people to go on dates with. Fair enough, I suppose.

In addition to lectures, I go to seminars. Seminars are like mini lectures. The lecture cohort is divided into smaller groups, and these groups attend seminars. Unlike in lectures – where it's the lecturer speaking to us – in seminars we get the chance to speak, expressing our views about what has been taught. In general, there is a lot more theory (to understand management) than practice (how 'to do' management), which I didn't expect. I guess I thought the process of managing others could be reduced to simple principles that I could memorise. I was wrong. How might we manage people in different cultures? And of different ages? How do we manage in times of crisis? These are the sorts of things we have begun to explore. You can go quite deep into these questions when you start thinking about them and reading around them. As time passes, I hope to be able to tell you more about business school.

Outside of studying management, I joined the university rugby club and that has been good for me. My social life revolves around the rugby club – playing games on Wednesday afternoons and training on other days. I tend to hang around with other lads who play rugby. It's pretty stereotypical: boozy, machismo and camaraderie. But it's who I am and what I've always done. I don't want to suddenly pretend I'm some renaissance intellectual because I enrolled here. It's probably the case that the club you join – if you join a club, you don't have to – will determine, to a large degree, the experience you will have if you come to a business school. The people you meet, the rhythm of your week outside of the course, where you socialise and even how you dress will all be determined by the university clubs you engage with.

There is a university club or society for everything and everyone, from chess clubs to student politics clubs. From debating clubs to religious societies and singing, music and drama clubs. I have experience of three university clubs/societies. One – the rugby club – is my world. The other – a debating and politics club – is my girlfriend's. A third, student journalism, is something a friend of mine is dipping his toe into. I'll try and tell you what I've observed about these clubs, as I think doing so might help you conceptualise some of the social dimensions of university life.

Debating and politics clubs in my experience tend to attract students who are highly passionate and opinionated. They are somewhat tribal, seeing the world in a somewhat black-and-white way, believing 'our' politics are right and virtuous, while 'their' politics are wrong, even immoral. These clubs meet and have drinks and discuss things like tax and foreign policy! They may debate, with each other and other political clubs. These debates may even be judged and prizes may be handed out. There are clear differences between those on the left and right of university political societies and clubs. Politics at university is notoriously ruthless and cut-throat. If you're interested in politics, you might immerse yourself in this world.

Student journalists typically write for student newspapers and often focus on the antics of those in political and debating societies and sports clubs. If there have been scandalous and salacious things going on, they love it! They will write about it. I guess they really want to publish stories in the national press, if they can. Not just the student newspapers. Like those who debate and join political societies, student journalists might see their involvement and experiences at university as launchpads into 'proper' grownup careers. My girlfriend is very active in the politics society. She seems to be using her time at university to position herself for a career in politics. Likewise, my friend who writes for the paper says he will keep all the stories and articles he writes and present them later, when he applies for jobs. I guess engaging with these societies represents extra-curricular activities that can benefit you later in life. Personally, I find politics and journalism boring. I'd rather hit rucks and go for beers with the lads afterwards.

Sports clubs are varied. There is a diverse set of clubs and even clubs within clubs. If you're talking about people at the elite level, they are going to play sport professionally after university or may already be playing sport professionally while at university. So, there is real diligence and professionalism displayed by these students, akin to an Olympic athlete. The rowers for example: they are up and on the river every morning at 6 am. They are in the gym five times a week. They follow very strict diets. You never see them out in the kebab shops I frequent at 2 am after a night out. But there is a spectrum, from people doing university sports in ways that mean sport is the centre of their university life to people who play sports casually. For some sports clubs, there has traditionally been a 'boozy' dimension associated. This is perhaps dissipating, and the extreme rituals (e.g. initiation ceremonies for new ruby players) that once underpinned university sport are disappearing. I guess that, because you're sporty, you'll gravitate to a university sports club if you come to business school. I think that'll be good for you. There might be a first, second and third team for the sport you play – so as you get older and bigger and better at your sport, you might play at a higher level.

I think it's important to point out that away from your course, there are opportunities for you to develop interests and meet like-minded people. Part of the university is experimenting with who you are (and who you are not). Clubs and societies allow this to occur. It's important to be yourself. There is, I feel, a clear social hierarchy at university; or at least a clear hierarchy in terms of how the sporting clubs organise themselves. It seems that students who went to very prestigious boarding schools are normally 'at the top' of the social hierarchy. This puts pressure on some to emulate these people, in terms of how they talk and dress. I'm not sure this is healthy. I hear people with strong regional accents in fresher's week trying to affect BBC pronunciation by the second or third week of study. Is that authentic? Or is that just fitting in and a process of becoming? Even worse, perhaps: I see students from very affluent backgrounds trying to disguise their back-grounds, dressing like they're homeless and using slang. Again, this might be read as amounting to deception (of self and others) and can't be a healthy long-term bet for your mental health and development. However, it can also be read as experimentation and part of becoming. My advice? Don't try to fit in. Just find your people and allow a fit to materialise. You will grow and evolve naturally, not in contrived ways that are rooted in styles and fashions rather than substance.

So, I would say – yes – come to university and be aware of the opportuni-ties it will give you, both in and outside of the lecture hall. Be aware that clubs and societies exist, and there are social and cultural 'rules' and 'norms' to take into account in terms of who joins them and how to act when in them. As for me, right now I am happy and in the moment. I am feeling a sense of freedom, no longer living in a small town I found to be suffocating and judgemental. Instead, I am living in the middle of a campus near a major city and feel like I'm making friends for life. I have faith that all the dots will join, during and after my course. Some days, I wake up and walk down the street with so much confidence and swagger and feel like I'm me for the first time in my life. I feel like there are so many opportunities coming my way. Perhaps, I am kidding myself.

Feel free to email me again in the future, when I might be able to tell you more about what to expect.

Titus

Summary of Key Points

- Business schools are unique within universities. A large number of subjects are taught in a business school.
- Business schools should focus on making you 'employable'; but that is not the same thing as spoon-feeding you some imagined formula or set of rules that you simply have to rote learn and reproduce after studying.
- You should feel that you will have options when you complete your degree.
- Choose a business school in the sort of geographical and cultural context that suits you as an individual, where you will 'fit in' and also grow.
- University is not for everyone – don't feel forced to study higher education if it's not right for you.
- Outside of your studies, at universities, there are lots of exciting opportuni-ties and activities for you to pursue.

Exercises/Questions for Discussion

- Every degree course requires the student to take charge of their own learning, and to be independent – are you ready for that?
- Is there a particular career or job you have in mind for when you graduate?
- How will a degree help you achieve this career goal?
- What is the most useful piece of advice Eve offers, in your opinion?
- What is the most useful piece of advice Titus offers?

Glossary Terms

Business school: the school in a university that organises how those studying business are taught and assessed. Business schools are made up of academic staff who teach and research business, professional support staff who manage the school's administration and students studying. Business schools are normally housed in their own building.

Employability: the idea that students should study things that make them appealing to prospective employers in the future. These include hard skills (e.g. technical ability, such as in IT) and soft skills (e.g. looking and sounding the way employers expect).

Journal: an academic journal is a place where academics publish research. They can be located and read online. Part of the fees you pay to a university go towards giving students access to read journals, which charge subscribers.

Module: if your degree is a cake, a module is a small slice of the cake. You study a number of modules as part of your degree. Some modules are optional (you choose them) and others are compulsory (you must study them). Each module has an amount of 'credit' attached to it – you must study enough credits over your degree to be awarded your degree.

Open day: a day, or number of days, when the business school is open to guests – normally prospective students. Visitors can look around the school, meet current students and staff, learn more about the degree(s) offered and even attend introductory lectures.

Peer-reviewed research: the journals discussed above publish research – specifically peer-reviewed research. The people who teach you might try and publish research. They will submit research to journals. Other academics ('peers') will review the papers and suggest changes, (or reject the paper). Papers are reviewed by other academics (peers) to ensure they have sufficient quality and rigour.

Semester: a length of time within the academic year when teaching takes place. There are normally two main teaching semesters in the academic year, from fall to Christmas and then from the New Year to the Spring.

Seminar: a small group which sees people studying your module come together. In the seminar, discussions may take place. Activities may also happen, such as group work. The cohort who attends lectures will be divided into smaller groups, and meet in seminars.

2
BEING A BUSINESS STUDENT

Part One: Reading and Writing

Adam is now in his first term at business school. He writes to Eve again to ask her advice about what he should be doing, now that he is an undergraduate.

From: Adam
To: Eve
Subject: I made it!
Date: Year 1, Semester 1

Hi Eve,

Well, I did it – I applied to some business schools and managed to get in. And even more than that, I managed to get into my first-choice business school, which is where I am currently writing to you from. I'm about three or four weeks in, so I've had some introductory lectures. You're right – this is a fast-paced place. I'm familiarising myself with the building and the campus more generally. I am excited but slightly nervous. It's nice to send an email to you and think about how you probably felt similar to me when you started, and how you moved forward.

   Thanks for the emails you sent me last year. They answered so many of my questions and convinced me that attending a business school was the best option – though it was good to know that it wasn't the *only* option!

   I am really enjoying business school so far. Even if it's a little overwhelming at times. I miss school and home a little. I moved around an hour away

DOI: 10.4324/9781003467397-3

from where I grew up, to a relatively large city. But I'm getting more familiar with my new routine. I've met some really nice people. And I've already learned some interesting ideas. Some of the lecturers are so passionate and knowledgeable. Some seem conceited and pretentious. I guess it's a microcosm of life.

The first week was **fresher's week and induction**. That seems like a blur now. We then had some gentle, introductory **lectures** to help navigate us, focus us and prepare us for what is coming. It looks like I'm entering the cut-and-thrust of **semester 1** now. I expect the intensity to rise. They've already started talking about assessments, which are due after Christmas.

I hope you don't mind me emailing you again. As I said last time, I see you as someone on the inside and someone who has experience of what I'm going through. So, if I can draw on your experiences, I'll be so grateful. Nobody else in my family has ever been to a university so it really is quite alien to me. I realise it'll take me a long time to learn all I need to know, and that I don't need to know everything now. But it'll be good to get a more general understanding of what my aims should be now and how I can think about and conceptualise some of the new but vital information coming my way, as I learn to be 'a student'.

After deciding to come to business school, I now have questions about what to do at business school. I don't mean at a subject level – I ended up studying a business and entrepreneurship degree, which has clear modules and is well-structured. I mean what to do in terms of managing my time on a day-to-day and week-to-week basis. (I must admit, I wasn't sure what you meant by 'modules' in your last email, but now I'm here I see what you mean: they are just smaller units of the degree, on specific subjects like introduction to business, introduction to enterprise and introduction to sales, with each module having its own lectures and assignment. Currently, I want to form my own business when I leave university, employ lots of people and grow a 'proper' business like the ones we've been learning about in the early lectures. This might seem like a lofty ambition and it's one I did not have before enrolling here. Maybe in time, I will realise this dream).

Anyway, hope to hear from you soon. I hope you're enjoying your second year. My Mum told me you'd enjoyed your first year immensely and did really well in all your assessments. A first, no less! That's amazing. Although I must confess I am not sure what a first means – though I do know it's really good. Keep up the good work, I guess!

Adam

Eve replies in the following email.

From: Eve
To: Adam
Subject: RE: I made it!

Hello Adam,

It's very nice to hear from you again. I am so happy for you. I think you made a great choice going to business school. I hope I didn't influence you too much or put you off other options. But I also hope I showed you what a business school might be like as an experience, so that you could decide what is best for you, at a personal level. It's always a good idea to get a general sense of what an experience might be like from someone who already has knowledge of that experience.

Yes, I got a 'first' in my first year. I now have to try and get a first in this – my second – year. A first means I averaged over 70% when they calculated all my modules together. Anything over 70% – including 70% – is a first. A first is the highest grade classification you can get. The 60s are a 2:1. Most people want (at least) a 2:1 as that is considered a very respectable classification and the level needed for entry into (most) graduate training schemes with major firms. It is also the level normally required to study for further degrees, like master's degrees. If you're in the 50s is a 2:2. If you average in the 40s, you get a third. A third is the lowest classification. Less than 40 is a failure. Ironically, my first year doesn't count towards my final **degree classification**. I only needed to pass the first year (with more than 40%) to progress to year two. It is the modules in years two and three that count to my final degree. In other words, it's what my average grade turns out to be over years two and three that will determine my final, 'real' degree classification. And even then, there is nuance, with my second-year average constituting 40% of my final grade and my third-year average contributing a massive 60%. So, on one hand, the first I got is meaningless in terms of final degree classification. How I do in years two and (especially) three is more important. On the other hand, I'm really proud to have averaged a first in year one.

You might ask why the degree classification is calculated in this way. By the way, this structure which sees students 'only' need to pass year one and then acquire their degree classification in years two and three is not specific to my business school but typical of almost all business schools in the UK – all my friends at other business schools are undergoing the same thing. I guess year one is about ensuring all people are capable of progressing to year two. Some will be, some will need more time. Year one is in place to allow those who need more time to 'get up to speed' to do so. It gives them space to learn the skills they need. It gives those who have those skills already more time to hone them. Likewise, in terms of the question, 'why does year three carries more weight in terms of degree classification?', I asked a lecturer about this and she said it is because the level of study is more demanding, and the assessments are designed to be more challenging. So, doing well in your third year requires more skills and craft, and the way your degree is classified in terms of the attribution of grades reflects this. In terms of my own journey, there are all sorts of advantages in getting a first in year one. Such as an increase in self-confidence. Also, the point of year one is to make sure I have the skills – or help cultivate the skills – needed to do well in years two and three. So, figuring out why I got a first in year one is useful as it might help me retain that level. For students who didn't do as well, figuring out why (and fixing it) is important, as that is the only way they can bolster their grades in the future.

I think your question about time management is very relevant. If I did well last year, it's probably because I was able to manage my time. This is not a skill I had before coming to university, but it's a skill that is obviously important in life and one I will try and cultivate further. I didn't read any books to help me 'learn' to manage my time. I just sort of followed my instinct and common sense to ensure the time I had was used well. In the context of my degree, time seems so abundant during some periods (we seem to have so much time that we waste it) and yet at other times, it seems like there are not enough hours in the day, and some course mates are scrambling to get key bits of work done by certain deadlines. There is a tendency for some students to do little to no work for weeks – except for maybe attend lectures, even though they may zone out when they're there. Then, these students must suddenly put assignments together, going over weeks of reading they should have done and trying to synthesise all of that reading into a cohesive assignment. Last-minute work reads like last-minute work and is unlikely to get a high grade.

The truth is that, for the vast majority of the semester, there should be time to work and play. You shouldn't ever feel stretched and under severe pressure to meet deadlines, and you shouldn't ever be feeling bored and that there's nothing to be doing. I'm not saying this is what happens. But I am saying that a well-structured degree will have a steady stream of work for you to do throughout, and spread-out deadlines. It is up to you to manage time and work within this structure. I guess – going back to your question on 'independent learning' –this is what a university means by independent learning: you must learn independently in the sense that you must choose when to learn (and to an extent what to learn).

It may sound simple and obvious, but I strongly suggest the following practical acts in terms of helping you manage time or more accurately manage learning over time: attend your lectures and seminars. And listen when in them. But also read after the lectures and in between lectures. What does this mean more specifically? At the end of each lecture, there will be suggested reading, on a **reading list** (it might be called mandatory reading or something similar). Simply read what is suggested on a week-to-week basis. You'll be amazed at how much knowledge you accumulate doing this. The reading lists should be manageable. They should keep you busy, but not so busy the amount of reading you do is overwhelming. Consistent learning – a little every day, or so (let's be realistic) – is a better strategy than 'cramming' at the end. Don't read obsessively and fanatically. Just read enough to know what is going on a week-to-week basis. As well as learning this is good for your mental health, it's important to feel like you're always developing, always getting a little better. The antithesis is the anxiety that comes with feeling left behind, overwhelmed and like you're losing control.

Let me know if there's anything else I can help you with – always happy to impart my great wisdom! ☺

Eve

From: Adam
To: Eve
Thanks, Eve.

I'm also after some advice on getting the most out of lectures and seminars and picking your brains more on 'independent study', which you mentioned in your last email, and which is something I heard a lot about during induction and my first lectures, but which I've not as yet embraced as a concept. It seems like the onus is going to be on me, as a student, to read, think and write 'independently'. Aren't I supposed to reproduce what others have said? That was the model at school, and I am not sure if I want to deviate from that. I am comfortable with it. It's not like I'm suddenly going to become some genius businessman overnight – isn't it the case that the best I can hope for, as a student, is to paraphrase the work of other people?

Adam

From: Eve
To: Adam

Hi Adam,
No, I don't think being a student is just about paraphrasing or parroting things you read or hear in lectures – although I do see how it might seem like that. At school, there was always a 'right' answer, wasn't there? The teachers at school had the job of getting everyone in the class to know the things that were on the syllabus by the end of the academic year. University is different. Yes, lectures and the recommended reading will present the points of view of your lecturer and the authors they think are worth reading – but these should be the starting point for your own thought, not the be-all-and-end-all of the topic under discussion.

When you're reading, try and make it as 'active' as possible. Highlight the most important, significant bits of what you read and make notes, so you can return to this reading in the future and 'do things' with it. Ideally, when reading, have a copy of the assessment criteria with you. What does this mean? As well as a reading list, your module leader should give you an idea of what the assignment is asking you (assessment criteria). This will include the word count, the date the assessment is due and how/where to submit the assessment. Ideally, the module leader will publish the module's assessment criteria early on in the module. The assessment criteria will specify the question being set (always answer the question set!) and will typically have a marking criterion included with it. If it's an essay or a report, read suggested reading while considering the set question in mind. In other words, read while thinking 'how does what I'm reading relate to what I'm being asked?' 'How can this information be used in a way that will help me answer the set question?' That way, when you identify information through your reading that will help you address the question, highlight that information with a view to using it in the future. For example, if you read an article and it explains that there are three main theoretical ways to look at a debate (then the article gives references to key scholars in these areas and names and explains these three ways and their differences) and the set question is asking you about this debate, it is obviously worth your while highlighting this information, then using it in the assessment. You might even read the references given.

On the basis of your reading, you can then say something like:
'when looking at debate x, we can view it through three distinct lenses. Lense A sees the debate y. Past work using this lens includes E, and has

discovered F. In contrast Lense B views the debate XX. Past work using this lens has shown G (references). Lense C is more concerned with Z. The main theorists who have contributed to this perspective include FF and GG. The main differences between the perspectives are E. In particular, Lense A has been criticised for being too extreme and ignoring the G aspects of B and C'.

This is obviously hypothetical and is being used to make a point. But, hopefully, you can see how a command of literature – that is an understanding of what has been said – allows you to display knowledge and 'anchor' your discussions. Let's say that you decide to evaluate the debate through an opinion that claims C is 'correct' or most promising. An evaluation like that is considerably more creditable (and likely to get a good grade) if it has a sound discussion before it, showing the writer has understood and contextualised the polemic and allowing the assertion to be rooted in extant thought and accepted, conventional academic scholarship.

Likewise, if your **assignment** is asking you a question and you read statistics and a key case study into the area as part of your reading, obviously it's a good idea to highlight this information and return to it in the future. You can then say something like:

'when studying x' (with x being the 'thing' that the assessment is asking you about), statistics show us y (sales in this area have steadily increased, and they especially increased in 2014). This matters because x is a 'growth market' that we might exploit. It is not a declining area – generally, it is not worth spending resources on an area that is declining and is likely to be loss-making. That said, it is likely to be a market that others will look to exploit, which means we must act in certain ways. Indeed, case ER is important as when they launched product CA in 2014, sales in the market increased dramatically, as figure 1 shows. We may look to mimic what ER did, but in ways that are more innovative. Specifically, we will …. '

This sort of information helps you give context to and frame an essay and roots what you're discussing in relation to relevant, existing literature. This is the sort of stuff you need to do for a good grade to emerge. It shows original thought and strategic planning, but also how that thought and planning is intrinsically linked to past events and perspectives, which you're displaying knowledge about.

Eve

From: Adam
To: Eve

Thanks Eve, that's really helpful.

I think I'm still a bit worried about how much there is a 'right' answer that the lecturer or TA who is looking for. Like, there's a girl in one of my seminars who the TA just seems to love, because she always says things that agree with whatever we just heard in the lecture. I'm not saying she's not clever or that she hasn't done the reading, because she clearly is, and has. But what if I really don't agree with the party line? Am I going to get marked down for not agreeing?

Adam

From: Eve
To: Adam

Don't worry, I think we've all met people like that girl! But I'm sure you wouldn't be marked down for disagreeing. I mentioned '**marking criteria**' before. My lecturers provide a grid – a sort of rubric – that explains how they will grade the assignments they've set you. I get the feeling that these are a general guide and shouldn't define your essays, but – for students like us – they are helpful to think about when reading around your essay (and planning your essay). Bear the criteria in mind; if for no other reason than when you get your grade back if you've done what was asked but failed to get the grade you expected, you can ask why and demonstrate why the case may be higher (in your view), showing how your assessment complies to what was being asked.

Normally, a marking grid will stipulate that a large percentage of the grade you get will be given for 'analysis' and 'engagement with reading/wider literature'. Therefore, if you do what I suggest above in terms of using what you read to analyse *in your* assignment and *frame your* assignment, you're more likely to do a lot of what the criteria are telling you to do. The criteria reflect what a good essay does. A good essay therefore reflects the criteria. (Coincidentally, concluding well, introducing well, referencing well and structuring the assignment well are normally other things the criteria will specify as required for a higher grade, that is a grade in the mid to high 60s and 70s).

I've said that a good strategy is to read a little each week, ensuring you read the reading(s) that your module leader specifies. Then, when it's coming up to the assessment hand-in date, switch gears. By which I mean, when it comes to the time to *plan your assessments* and *write up material that will be assessed*, go from a steady state of acquiring information via reading to focusing on finding and utilising more specific sorts of information, ensuring you can do what you need to with that information. Namely use it to get good grades, within a well-structured and well-planned assessment that answers the question you've set in a style and structure that is not rushed and which has a clear, cohesive narrative. As discussed above, by highlighting, ordering and managing information you've read in the past, the act of doing this in the present – or at the key time when writing assignments – is much easier.

Having, firstly, read then, secondly, written up what you've read in an assignment, keep going over drafts of the essays, reports etc. that you're being asked to write, making sure you answer what is being asked and that your answer is formed in a way that uses what you've been taught and what you've read. All that learning – in this case, all that reading to supplement lecture slides – is used to evidence and back up what you say in assignments. Show you've understood. However, and this is crucial, don't try and synthesise all you've read into the assignment. Much of what you've read may be irrelevant. Take command of what you've read to form an answer – don't let what you've read command you, allowing you to get lost in it, and going off on points that seem relevant but – with closer inspection via *editing* (more on that below) – prove to be irrelevant in this context. There is simply too much information at the university level to try and include everything, or even most of what you've learned. Answer a specific area in detail. It is for this reason that some module leaders give students a choice of things to write about – several topics are presented as ones you can choose to write about. This way students can look at one topic in detail at the level of assessment while also learning about other areas that interest them, but which are not directly linked to their assessment.

I'll now try and demonstrate some points about editing – that is drafting and redrafting what you write. This is a process, and a key process. It's unlikely that what you write early on when writing an assessment is what you'll hand in (unless you're very short on time). Rather, you will keep revisiting what you write and developing it, in ways that mean it acquires more grades (i.e. in ways that make what you write analytical, rooted in wider thought, answers the set question and does any other things stipulated on the assessment criteria). Let's say that you're writing about why marketing is important and how you'd market a product. Let's say you write something like this (note, I've purposefully not used references here and I'm writing simplistically to make my point):

'it's important to market products and services. If I was going to market, I would try and create an advert that appeals to people. I would be careful to ensure those doing the marketing are managed correctly. If they are not managed correctly, they may lose morale. They may go and work for a rival'

You then revisit this section and realise it can be edited, for three reasons and in three ways. You think, first – let's substantiate the original point about the importance of marketing – it's too general. It needs editing. Second, let's make the point about constructing an advert more specific. This is an important point that I can add to. Third – and this is more important – while the discussion about the management of others might be interesting in and of itself, is it actually relevant to the question being asked? No! So take it out. Editing is about improving what is already there if it answers the question and also taking stuff out that does not answer the question. If the question was 'is managing markets important?', then you could use it (as a base for further editing). But that is not the question here in this hypothetical scenario. So we delete it. We always ensure what we write is relevant. At first, I found this odd – it felt like a waste. I'd tell myself 'But I've spent time writing that!' or I'd convince myself 'it's relevant'. But as time passed, I started realising the value of deleting anything that is not focused. Be laser-like. Be brutal as an editor. You can always use 'track changes' if you're editing on Microsoft Word. This is helpful in the editorial process.

So – in italics – we edit by adding the following points. Simultaneously, we delete from 'I would be careful' to 'rival' because – although it sounds good – it does not address what is being asked directly. So, after reading and reflecting on what you've written, you edit – that is improve – the essay by simply adding something like this:

'it's important to market products and services. *Billions of pounds are spent on advertising and marketing, and degrees are taught because marketing skills are in demand. Marketing can be the difference between realising growth and failure. Indeed, business history shows that the most innovative marketing often leads to the most fruitful outcomes in terms of sales and brand image.*

If I was going market, I would try and create an advert that appeals to a specific stratum of people. This is because we know that adverts which try to appeal to too many people are unlikely to be noticed, liked by – and conducive to prompting sales from – customers who want and need what you're selling. Budget levels, age, geography, gender and social class all impact what people want to buy and the extent to which an advert appeals to them. For example, an advert for a luxury perfume targets a different audience than an advert for a lawnmower. I'd use different marketing techniques – such as visuals and audio – to appeal to the specific strata of people who may be interested in what I'm selling'.

Note the way that, after the edit, what was one paragraph before containing two points (on (a) the importance of marketing and (b) how I'd market) becomes two paragraphs, with each paragraph focusing on one point in more detail. This is basic editing. But it's a skill that will be invaluable to you, as you look to adjust to university (and life after). You can make points more succinctly and clearly. You don't have to be a great writer, but you can be a very solid writer if you learn to edit and focus your paragraphs on a specific point and allow all the paragraphs to come together and answer what is being asked (and only what is being asked).

A key tip: attend **assessment workshops** if they are offered, in the weeks before assessments are due. These workshops are where you get to show plans of assessments to your lecturers and get feedback. Speak to your lecturers directly to get a sense of what they want and the extent to which your work adheres to this. I think my assignments improved by at least 5% – 10% when I attended workshops in my first year. I got help with how to structure my work and also learned about specific journal articles I was not aware of but which really helped locate my arguments and the lines of thought I was going down. The best plan is to go to as many workshops as possible, taking work and allowing the lecturer to explain how your work can evolve on a week-to-week basis. Establish an honest, open dialogue with the lecturer. Don't be offended if their feedback appears negative! They are just doing their job, giving you honest feedback, which you can use to produce a better final assignment.

By doing the above, you will not have to stress about producing work at the last minute, and you should avoid that unhealthy and unproductive pattern of periods of too little followed by periods of too much. Like I said, work produced too late reads like that – hurried work that lacks robustness. It's unlikely to get you the top grades. Even if you're doing part-time paid work outside of your degree (and you might have to limit paid work around university assessment deadlines), the approach described here will, in general, allow you to manage your time and find that important balance between producing but not being overwhelmed.

Eve

From: Adam
To: Eve

Thanks again, Eve. Can I just ask how did you find your end-of-first-year exams? I'm trying not to think about them yet, but I must admit I sometimes feel a bit worried about what they'll be like. I found A levels quite tough, to be honest, so the thought of having more exams next summer is not filling me with joy!

Adam

From: Eve
To: Adam

Ah yes, exams: those dreaded, unseen questions which are becoming quite uncommon in university business schools today, and which students typically dread, but which can be managed in ways akin to the above. In exams, get a general sense of what will come up. Read around it. Make visuals that allow you to reproduce key information (e.g. key studies) in the exam. Respond to what is being asked on the day. Write specifically in relation to it. Stay calm. You can't edit and re-edit in an exam. But you can go in with a lot of knowledge memorised and a determination to plan before you start, and therefore give yourself a good chance of responding to the question. Exams tend to be marked more generously than written assignments, in my experience.

You asked about lectures and seminars, and I mentioned those a little above. Let me say more on those now. Think of lectures as navigation. The lectures should be structured in a way where you learn specific aspects of what the module aims to teach you, over time. Each lecture should be about a particular theme or issue and have a reading list attached to it. Read, as discussed above! The best lecturers will explain why what you're learning is relevant to 'the real world' but also your assessment. So, when you're in lectures, think 'what information is being taught here that I can use or might need to use later, when I have to submit an assessment?' This goes back to the principle of highlighting key information when reading and separating highly relevant information and relevant information from what is otherwise a huge surplus of information: all of which can't and shouldn't be entirely engaged with. Let the lectures navigate you, as a series of integrated stages. Lectures often have 'learning goals' and 'learning aims' in bullet points at the start of them. Remember these during lectures – there should be a point – that is a clear focus and narrative or story – to the seemingly endless slides and talking! In short, use lectures as a way to figure out what information you need – and how to present that information – to get you 'bang for your buck' when getting grades.

Lectures at business schools are often attended by lots of – sometimes hundreds of other – students, as you'll have found out. There should be a little bit of time left at the end of the lecture for questions. I urge you to spend some time asking your lecturer questions at the end of the lecture if you are confused or even if you're enthusiastic and want to express that and especially if you want to learn more! You might also pick up some key – otherwise elusive – information from your lecturer when you engage with them, which might be useful at a later point. Because so many people attend lectures, students are probably somewhat anonymous to the lecturer, especially over the first few weeks of a module. Getting to know the lecturer can be a good move, as you can help settle them as well as settle yourself. Now if a lecturer can't answer a question at a set point or says something like 'in a few weeks that will become clear', trust the process! You can always revisit the question at a later point if things don't become clearer.

While I think it's good to get to know your lecturers, remember that lecturers are not there to be your friends! They are there to teach you and assess you. They will assess your work anonymously – they mark assessments without a sense of who the student is. There is no bias. It's not a popularity contest. So, see them for what they are – human beings who have the same insecurities and weaknesses as other humans! But humans who should know a lot about what they are teaching and what you are learning and who are resources for you to learn from. Lectures are generally scheduled to occur for an hour. You'll probably find lecturers talking for 45 minutes and then leaving time for questions. Sessions should not exceed what is scheduled. I heard somewhere that attention spans go after minutes. The lecturer should get key points across early in their teaching, before we, as students, zone fully out.

Seminars are smaller than lectures in terms of the number of students attending. The best seminars will see you and other students discuss areas linked to lectures. These discussions should supplement your learning, building on what you learn in lectures and from your own studying and reading outside of teaching hours. That said, don't give all your best ideas away in seminars! Others might copy them! To a large extent, how lively and interesting seminars are will depend on who you happen to have alongside you in your seminar group. Some groups may be quieter and therefore less engaging. This is a reflection of the personalities in the seminar group. Some seminar groups may have students who try and dominate discussions. (A good seminar leader will do their best to suppress these students, while not excluding them, and also try and encourage more introverted, less vocal students to contribute.) Who knows where the spectrum will be in your seminar groups. A good seminar leader will manage you through it. To repeat: use time in seminars to get clarity on key aspects of the module's wider assessments and learning goals.

When the lockdowns happened, universities had to respond quickly in terms of implementing **online learning resources** for students. (e.g. lectures were recorded and uploaded). These online infrastructures are still largely in place and can help you further when navigating information. Don't be afraid to ask to utilise these opportunities, if they're accessible and if your lecturers don't mind sharing them. (If they do, don't keep pestering! You don't want to seem like you're demanding and expect). As well as your lecturers, you will have a degree director and a senior tutor. (Some universities also implement personal tutors to oversee your pastoral, as distinct from academic, needs). It might be an idea to speak to these people about accessing online resources. Also, it's good to speak to these people if problems emerge. For example, your degree director is a good person to raise observations and even complaints you have, for example, if there's a problem with teaching or workload. If you need to travel or get ill or some close relation or friend dies, these people are important ones to tell and engage with and seek advice from, ensuring you comply with university regulations and appropriate practices; for example, to get extensions in place.

Anyway, I hope this all helps?!

Have a lovely day.
Eve

Part Two: Living the Life

As he did last time, Adam writes to Titus as well as Eve to get further information. Adam's correspondence with Titus is centred on his lifestyle and lifestyle choices, and how these relate to studying, learning and thriving at a business school.

From: Adam
To: Titus
Subject: I made it.
Time: Semester 1 Year 1

Hi again!
I was hoping to catch up with you over the summer when you came home. But apparently you spent all summer laying bricks?! Anyway, you might have heard that I am at university now studying entrepreneurship. I found your last email

very helpful, Titus. You might remember that you wrote to me when you were in your first year. I wonder if you can advise me further, now that I'm a first year and you're a second year and you've gained even more experience of how to navigate and survive a business school, which I can draw on. This time I'd like to know more about what to do practically at an everyday level. I want to use my time outside of university to be 'my best self'. I've been here a few weeks now and I worry that I am in danger of just 'following the crowd', that is just doing the same as everyone else, mainly because I don't have a plan. When I think of you, I think of someone who stands out, someone who doesn't just blindly follow. That is a good thing! Nobody has ever taught me the skills of how to live well. I find I am drifting sometimes: eating junk, staying up late, not really engaging with what I'm being taught. Have you any prescriptions about how to cultivate a routine or framework, in which I can live in a way that gives me the best chance of developing as a scholar and a person? In some ways, I feel like learning these skills will be one of the most important lessons I learn at university.

All the best,
Adam

Titus responds in the following email.

From: Titus
To: Adam

Hi there Adam. Thanks for emailing me. It's always nice to hear from you and I really enjoy emailing you as it helps me focus my own thoughts and outline my experiences in ways that are helpful. There's something about articulating, in words, what you know to be true that makes you think more profoundly and makes those truisms somehow more real. Anyway, to answer your email, Yes, I stayed here all summer, near the university. I am renting a house with a group of friends next year. We will all live together in the second year. It's a dirty, overpriced house in the heart of the student area. It's perfect. I got to live in the house on my own for the summer. It was lonely sometimes. I didn't come 'home', back to the old town. I spent the summer laying bricks. It got me fit, and I made lots of money. I saved most of the money I made.

Most students left **campus** and the city. So, I was in our student house by myself for six weeks. I socialised with 'new people' – that is people not at the university. Not people who come and live here for a few years, before moving to a place to do a 'graduate job'. I'm talking about people who were born and raised here, and who will probably live here for most of their lives. They work hard, they make little and their options are few. It was refreshing to hear their views. It also showed me how international and wide my views, experiences and skill sets are – university and business school are very important in teaching a way of seeing the world. What opportunities we have, just by enrolling. Don't take the opportunities that you can fashion for granted. Overall, I am pleased I have experienced the summer I have. But I don't want to look down on those who were less fortunate and I certainly don't want to discredit the views of others, though they are different to mine. I hope I don't see my way – 'our way' – of looking at things as inherently better or more enlightened, even if our ways are the established, accepted ones in the seats of learning. I think that at the start of the summer, I was possibly guilty of looking down on others, and sure I was 'right'. I am no longer inclined to think this way. I realised I'm a very young person with a small range of experiences, especially compared with some of the people I met and worked with.

I said it was a lonely time, but it was also a formative time. I learned loads. There is something about solitude and daily routine that gives one the space and time to think, learn and grow. I guess we live in such a fast, superficial world now. There is pressure to always be doing some new thing, in some new way; moving from one thing to the next and one place to another. Actually, I found that within the apparently mundane – that is within the daily structure of get up, go to work, come home and read repeat rhythm – there was a peace and security I enjoyed. There were also opportunities to develop – indeed there wasn't much else to do! By not having my friends around me constantly and just doing what they wanted, I was able to grow as a person. I didn't feel pressure to be 'like them'; I felt like I could be me. I became a bit more independent. I feel like I've grown into 'the real me', or the version of me I think I'll become. In fact, I learned a lot about cultivating the sorts of habits and incorporating the sorts of 'life lessons' you mentioned in your email into my daily routine.

I learned this stuff from reading – and reading books that you won't find on most university reading lists. I also learned this stuff by listening to one or two older heads I met on the building site. Who'd have thought, I come to a prestigious seat of learning and its brickies whom I learn some of the best lessons from! So, I'll now tell you what I learned, how I learned it and what it all means for you as a student and – maybe more importantly – for you as a person. A lot of it is intuitively true, but unless it's articulated, it can be hard for this 'truth' to be realised and implemented into everyday life. But I must emphasise that what suits one might not suit another. What I say below is stuff that has helped me, and is helping me reach my potential. But it might not suit you. We are all different and all must find what works for us. So, lessons I learned from my summer:

Lesson 1. Sleep is the foundation of life. I know that culture might glamorise a lack of sleep, and we hear phrases like 'sleeping is cheating'. Being up late is something of a rite of passage for students. But I read a book – Matthew Walker's *Why We Sleep* – and I learned so much. This isn't about how to fall asleep. It's a book about sleep from a scientific point of view, and how much we need it and what it does for us. I have incorporated sleep – what you might call 'sleep hygiene' which includes not looking at a phone or screen two hours before bed – into my life as a priority. I even bought a special pillow! However, this is not necessary. I went to bed at around the same time each night and got up at the same time each day. (In terms of the latter, I had to when I was working on the building site). What a difference consistency in sleep has made to me. By sleeping properly, I feel like I have developed some sort of superpower. Have a look at the notion of circadian rhythms. I believe my immune system is stronger and my mental health is stronger for it. Like I said, no screens before bed!

Lessons 2. Be hydrated and drink lots of water. Like sleeping, this is free and 'easy'. It's not complex or glamorous so might be rejected. Why is it that if something is complex and expensive, we are more likely to engage with it and take it seriously, but if something is basic – like sleeping more and drinking more water – we might dismiss it? Being hydrated is almost as important as being well-rested and having a good sleep routine. Our bodies are, after all, mainly water. Hydration is good for our health. It helps us think. I'm reliably informed it also makes us look healthier. Drink lots of water! Especially in the morning – after those hours of lovely sleep. Get up and drink a couple of pints of clean water straight away. You can add sea salt to your water if you want. It acts as an electrolyte.

Another thing that is free and might sound like I'm being flippant, but which I'm very keen to tell you about and which I suggest you incorporate in your everyday life, is breathing properly. This is distinct from just breathing. Like sleeping and being hydrated, think of breathing as an art form – something to work on and perfect; something to focus on when you wake up and throughout the day. So, lesson three is breathing through your nose, and breathing less often but breathing deeply. This will change your mood in an instant and over time will change your life, in ways you can't comprehend until you try it and read around it. Many good books have been published on breathing lately. Breathwork has become fashionable. I suggest reading Nestor's *Breath* as an introduction to the topic. Like Walker's book, discussed above in relation to sleeping, Nestor's work gets to the science around breathing, and how styles of breathing are more suited for different times (e.g. preparing for a big event, resting, decompressing before bed etc). There is a whole world of breathing for you to discover.

So a combination of consciously and systematically sleeping properly, breathing properly and staying hydrated will optimise your life. They are simple, foundational things which – if done properly – will cost you nothing financially but enable you to achieve so much. More importantly, they will make you feel differently and react to things differently – that is more healthily. You want these things to become habits. This will help give you the right mindset and state to achieve. But there are more lessons that I learned over the summer.

One of the people I used to lay bricks with swears by extremities of heat and cold, by which they meant using saunas and ice baths regularly. I must admit, I was sceptical at first. But again, there is hard science that shows the benefits of doing both of these things. Wim Hoff has popularised the latter. Cold water immersion is now mainstream. Though it's not without its controversy, critics and – at times – hyperbole. I now practice both, regularly. I hate getting into the cold water. But it turns out, that is a good thing. I learned about a thing called neuroplasticity from a brilliant scientist called Huberman (more on this below). When you do things you don't want to do – like hating the prospect of getting into the cold water but you go ahead and do it anyway – you change the way the brain is 'wired' and how it functions. You literally change who you are by forcing yourself to do things you don't want to do. You become a less fragile, more resilient self. So, doing the cold water has neurologically positive impacts! I joined a sauna. It's a cheap one. I like to go three times a week. Like the cold, the heat relaxes me. It's so important to find a way of dealing with the stresses of life. I would also include regularly stretching and exercising your body and walking in nature as further things you can do most days in order to give your mind and body the 'tools' they need to perform optimally and for a long period of time. You don't need to join an expensive gym! Learning to do calisthenic exercises in your house will do the trick! And nutrition is a huge part too – nutrition compliments all of these. Using supplements – like a general multivitamin or fish oil – can be a good and relatively cheap way of ensuring your body has the right nutrients in it while you're at university. Also, look into gut health. You want your guts to be healthy; for both optimal mind and body! Drinking Kombucha and eating fermented foods can help with this. Collectively, these constitute lesson 4: they are all focused on the body, but the truism a healthy body is a healthy mind is one to remember. You're more likely to concentrate, produce good work, have more energy, stay well and be happier by implementing these things. Actively take responsibility for your health. Imagine doing all of these things over a year – or multiple years – and then imagine how much better you will look and act in an interview and the world of work. Think of the implementation of the above as sound investments in you and your future.

Lesson 5 is to do with light, specifically the importance of getting daylight into your eyes as soon as you wake up. Don't look at the sun! But do get into the light as early as you can and let your body take in that light. This will regulate the circadian rhythm in your body (that is your natural body clock). This will have a profoundly positive impact on your life, including your sleeping patterns and energy levels. (Though in the UK, especially in the winter, it can be hard to get light in the mornings, but you can buy lights that do the trick through artificial light). I learned the importance of light from a scientific podcast by Huberman, whom I mentioned above, which is currently the world's number one health podcast. (Getting light first thing in the morning over the summer was easy, as I went to the building site when the sun was rising). The podcast is rooted in science and relies on peer-reviewed studies – not speculation – to make suggestions. You can learn so many tips from the podcast. So, a further lesson is to listen to high-quality podcasts that motivate and inform you in the same way that you should read books that have a similar positive and informing impact. Listen and learn from the experts. Don't be susceptible to any old rubbish and believe all you hear and read! Be discerning with the information you input. Even when reading and listening to what appears to be 'scientifically sound' sources like those above, always apply a level of discernment. Let your instincts and experiences use the information in ways that suit you, in a particular time and place.

When I was alone in the house after laying bricks all day, I grew to love the time I spent on my own, reading and listening to podcasts and learning and then making changes to my life to implement what I learned. What an advantage it has given me. I would have watched TV or wasted time. But without a TV or friends around, these options were taken from me. What a blessing in disguise. And that leads me to lesson 6, which is that time on your own is valuable and not to be avoided. Too many people need company. They avoid their own company. They will even spend time with people they don't like, just to not be alone. What a waste! Get used to spending time alone, learn to know yourself and find peace within. Don't rely on others. Even worse, some rely on others for 'friendship' and validation through social media. What a pernicious cycle to get into. If you can, get off social media. I did it, and I can't tell you how free I have found it – dealing with real life as it is in front of me, and with real people as they are, rather than a virtual, pretend world.

Lesson 7 is to do with saving. I think I told you in my last email that I was spending a lot of money. What a waste. Nobody has ever taught me anything about money – the importance of saving at least some of what I earn. The importance of not being in debt. Those bricks were heavy and the process of laying them was laborious. But I am now out of the debt I had got myself into and have put a little away for a rainy day. I met someone on the building site who claimed to be almost a millionaire just from saving smartly over a few years. It sounds farfetched. But I asked him his secret and he told me about the following book: *The Total Money Makeover* by Dave Ramsey. Having read this book, and having done the maths, anyone with an income can be rich, so long as they save, invest and don't take on debt. Avoid the concept of getting rich quickly. Switch to the notion of getting rich slowly (but surely). This requires investments and saving over time. This book will change your life financially, in the ways the lessons above will change your life in terms of health and fitness. Of course, while studying at a business school it is hard to save, I guess we are studying now to optimise our economic potential in the future. But once I realised that potential, I believe I now have the financial discipline and knowledge to make what I earn 'work for me'. I certainly don't want what I earn to simply service debt on things – like cars – I don't really need. You control your money, you control your life and – to an extent – this means you control your stress, which is my next lesson. Why is it that personal money management is not taught at schools and universities? As long as you're in debt, you'll always be living a form of slavery.

Lesson 8 is to do with stress. Limit stress: know what you can and can't control in terms of creating and dealing with stress. Some stress is inevitable and can't be avoided. It can be healthy and prompt you into action. See it as an inbuilt mechanism that can be your fiend. But too much stress or too much of the wrong sort of stress is deadly – it will sabotage how you think, feel and physiologically function in ways that are dramatic. A lot of stress, in my experience, is not 'real' but imagined: a result of chaotic thinking and assuming the worst. This sort of stress typically involves imagining an event in the future and thinking how bad things will be because of the event. The event is just imagined though. It almost certainly won't play out as you imagine. Don't think worrying about the future is productive or gives you any real control of a situation. Deal with facts. When there is a reason to stress, you'll be more resilient and resourceful than you might think! A lot of stress is also unnecessary and created through poor decisions we make or associating with the wrong people. Some people are just drama all the time. Do we need that in life? Finance and health problems are also causes of stress, especially later in life: but much of what I write about above will alleviate stress that derives from finance and health issues if implemented properly.

Like I said above, remember that stress – that is adrenaline or epinephrine – is a natural and to a point healthy response that your body produces. Fight or flight will save your life. But you don't want too much of it, or too much of it too often. I read a book recently, which a lecturer discussed when teaching, which has really helped me understand how my brain processes information, reacts to information and, in turn, causes 'stress'. The book has also given me a framework to help deal with stress; encouraging me to allow my 'human side' and not my 'chimp side' to be in control.

The book I'm talking about is titled *The Chimp Paradox*. It uses the metaphor of a Chimp to explain what is actually complex neuroscience, how our brains react to stimuli and which part of the brain we want to be functioning.

The premise of the book is as follows: we have a part of the brain (the chimp) which sees the world in black and white and is prone to chaotic thinking (stress) and other emotional reactions like anger and aggression. We have another part of the brain (the human) which is more rational, less emotional, less myopic and less vindictive than the chimp. In simple terms, the chimp is bad and the human is good. Road rage is a classic example. In the heat of the moment, rage rises up – our chimp is angry and reacts. In time, our human side kicks in and we reflect more logically; so, what if I was cut up in traffic? And, worse still, why did I react so disproportionately and in such an uncontrolled way? You can perhaps see the two sides of your brain and how one side – the chimp – may be hijacking you, and the need to manage your chimp. It's not just about driving. The principles apply to all aspects of life where emotions materialise and decisions have to be made.

We can't control the nature of our chimp but we must learn to control the chimp. We want the human part of the brain working for us, not the chimp. So, when you're processing information and feeling stressed and jumping to worst-case scenarios and conclusions, ask yourself is this really 'me' thinking this – the human – or my chimp? In time, when my human brain kicks in, might this situation look and feel different? Therefore, should I be sure not to act in a certain way now which I will regret. What a habit to cultivate. I am still working on this! Sadly, my chimp is still a dominant part of my thinking.

So you wanted life lessons to help you become 'the best version of yourself' so that you can achieve more with your work while at business school. You also wanted lessons to help you achieve outside of university, such as in future work roles and in everyday, seemingly mundane scenarios. Cultivate the habits or rules I've outlined over a lifetime: sleep properly and go to bed and wake up at the same time, be hydrated, breathe properly, use saunas and ice baths, enhance your life with exercise, a good diet and supplements, get natural light into your eyes first thing in the morning, read quality books and listen to quality podcasts, don't be afraid of – indeed embrace – time on your own, take control over your finances and use the metaphor of 'the chimp' to help understand and manage your thinking in order to reduce stress in your life. But the most important of all is sleep!

Inevitably, when you fail to do some (or maybe all) of these in a day, don't beat yourself up! It's an ongoing framework to guide your life. Also, remember that while these things work for me and are backed up with hard scientific findings (as well as anecdotal evidence), some might not necessarily work for you. We are all individuals on our own paths and must find out what works for us.

Anyway, must go – time for my ice bath!

Titus

Summary of Key Points

- Manage your time well throughout the year.
- It is the aim to grow as a scholar and a person.
- You should be learning consistently.
- You shouldn't be trying to 'catch up' later in semesters in order to construct assessments.
- Time spent reading – and using what you read – is vital.

Things to Think About

- How you live your life outside of studying has a dramatic impact on you and how you will feel and perform as a person and scholar.
- There are expectations or rules about how you are meant to present arguments and information at university – these rules can be learned and practised, like any skill. The better you are in terms of learning and applying these rules, the better you will do at the level of assessment.
- There are chances to develop your work with academics.

Exercises/Questions for Discussion

- Do you intend to incorporate any of Titus' lessons in your life? If so, which ones?
- In mind of Eve's discussion, list four things that you will do in order to give yourself the best chance of receiving high grades.
- How much time will you spend reading and how will you ensure you capture when reading has utility for you?
- As someone looking to learn, will you approach lectures and seminars differently? Why/why not?

Glossary Terms

Assignment: a piece of work that is used to assess a student.

Assessment workshops: a few weeks before assignments are due, a module may offer some assessment workshops, in which students can talk about the module's assessment in detail and perhaps share essay plans and get further suggestions on what to read.

Campus: the physical space that a university occupies in which its buildings and facilities are placed and located.

Degree classification: the degree a student is classified with at the end of their final year of study. The average grades gained in years two and three are used to classify the grade.

Fresher's week and induction: A fresher is a term that refers to somebody in their first year of studying at university. Fresher's Week is designed to integrate freshers into university life. It has become a predominantly social week, a rite of passage. Induction is a more formal, less social part of a fresher's early experiences of and integration into a university – it involves things like registering, meeting your lecturers and learning where relevant buildings exist and what is located in them.

Lectures: the process of learning that sees students congregate at a specific time and sit, while the lecturer guides them and teaches them.

Marking criteria: a list of things that somebody marking an assessment takes into account when allocating an assessment with a particular grade.

Online learning resources: any learning resource that students can access online, ranging from online access to books and journals to recordings of lectures.

Reading list: a list of reading composed by the lecturer to help students learn more about what is being taught. Reading lists will be mostly made up of books and, especially, journal articles.

Semester 1:   the first semester in the university year, normally running between September/October to January. Assignments will be set for the end of the semester. Those assignments will relate to things taught in semester 1. (it is followed by semester 2).

Further Reading

Nestor, J. (2020). Breath: The New Science of a Lost Art. Penguin.

Peters, S. (2012). The Chimp Paradox: The Acclaimed Mind Management Programme to Help You Achieve Success, Confidence and Happiness. Vermilion.

Ramsey, D. (2003). The Total Money Makeover: a proven plan for financial fitness. Thomas Nelson.

Walker, M. (2017). Why We Sleep: The New Science of Sleep and Dreams. Penguin.

3
ASSESSMENTS

Part One: Types of Assessments

Adam is approaching the end of his first year. He does not feel like he is in a strong and organised position to do well in his end-of-first-year assignments. In fact, he feels like he could fail his first year. He sends emails to Eve and Titus, asking for clarity.

From: Adam
To: Eve
Subject: End of year one stress and confusion/assessment deadlines
Time: Towards the end of semester 2 in year one

Dear Eve,

Well, here we are – past semester 1, into semester 2 and coming to the end of my first year! How time flies. Year one of my degree is coming to an end, which means the focus really switches to assessments – those end-of-semester assessments that count for about 70% of my first year and which I need to **pass and proceed** to year two. I'm about four weeks away from the point where most of my deadlines are clustered.

I'll be honest. I am struggling. I managed to pass most, though not all, of my semester 1 assignments. (No, I didn't attend the assessment workshops though I know you said I should have, and my course mates told me how helpful they were). But I mean 'passing' in the literal sense (just over 40%) rather

---

DOI: 10.4324/9781003467397-4

than in a way I would have liked. If truth be told, the situation I'm in is my own fault. As the weeks passed, my enthusiasm dissipated. I enjoyed lectures when I went (though I hardly went) and even, surprisingly, enjoyed doing semester 1 assessments when I actually started writing them and doing some work around them. ('Ah I see why they taught us this now', I used to think when writing, 'but I don't have the time or the knowledge to really use this material in a useful way'). I didn't attend enough, quite simply, and I left the process of writing my assessments to the very last minute. With one essay, I submitted moments before the deadline and didn't even complete my conclusion and **bibliography** – what the heck are bibliographies anyway?

I got into a routine of focusing too much on, let's say, extracurricular activities, rather than academic ones. I had lots of fun. That's sort of what the first year is for, I thought. But now I realise there's a balance between work and play. I probably started spending time with one or two people I shouldn't have – fun people, but people who aren't really in my corner and who aren't conducive to me moving forward and who aren't really rooting for me or concerned with my well-being – they are more concerned about how they can benefit from me. More honestly, I'm quite disappointed as I asked for your advice and then failed to implement it. Sorry! But I can still pass the first year, and – if I do – I promise I will try harder in year two. I can also **resit** some modules in the summer if I need to – but I obviously don't want to be doing this.

Apologies for another email. But I need all the help I can get at this point, as the deadlines approach and the pressure is ramping up and the gaps in my knowledge become all the more evident. Last week I started trying to get organised and plan which assessments I'll do and when – I have two **exams**, one **report**, two **essays** and a **presentation**. The presentation is a group-based one. I think the group are quite annoyed with me as I've not really turned up to their meetings and they seem to be working hard on 'our' presentation, in my absence. One said he was sick of the group 'carrying me'. Harsh?

The other two things I need advice on: writing and analysis. These are terms I hardly understand. I thought I knew what they meant. But it seems those assessing my work have a clear view of what the terms mean. And simply, I'm not doing what they want.

One lecturer said, to get a sense of where you are as a student and ascertain your ability, look across how you did in all your modules. That way you can get a more consistent, representative feel for the level you're at. This is instead of looking at the best grade you got in one module and thinking that one grade is representative of where I'm at. After all, the one grade in isolation can be anomalous. Looking across modules is more representative. In terms of numbers, when I look across my spread of grades in all the assessments I completed in semester 1, I'm pretty much consistently in the (low) 40s, with one module in the low 50s. I got **feedback** on all the grades I got back. This feedback is helpful. It gives a level of context to the number. There was a chance to see my lecturers about my grade – I wish I'd done that now, to get more detail about why I got the grades I did. When I deconstructed the feedback and looked for the reasons given as to why I got the grades I did, the aspects that always came up were writing style and lack of analysis. Another factor some lecturers gave for my poor performance was 'being too descriptive'. Maybe it's personal – maybe they don't like me?

I've tried to be as organised as possible, as I move forward. Before I sent this message, I started making a list of when everything is due and the titles of the assessments. This is a step forward for me. I can see there is quite a range of assessments – three essays, one report, one written exam and one presentation. Any advice on tackling the different sorts of assessments I have? In terms of the presentation, it is a group presentation where the marks are given to a group of students. There are five of us in the group. Like I said, the other members seem quite off with me. I've not turned up to the joint meetings they organised. They seem to have worked hard on the presentation so far, and probably think I've not pulled my weight – which I've not!

Anyway, hope all is well for you?! Hopefully see you over the summer, and I've not been kicked out of business school. I've tried to paint an honest picture of where I'm at and the particular challenges I face. My friend Titus told me about a book called *The Chimp Paradox*. Have you read it? I'm trying to let my human side control, not the chimp. Right now, the chimp is anxious! My friend also told me how important it is to breathe properly. I am trying to do this, and I must admit that 20 minutes or so of focused breathing really helps me.

I wish I could turn the clock back and listen to you. I don't want to fail the first year. I appreciate your time.

Adam

This is the email that Adam received from Eve, in response to his email.

From: Eve
To: Adam
Subject: RE: End of year one stress and confusion/assessment deadlines

Hi Adam. It sounds like you've enjoyed your time so far, at least socially if not academically. Don't be too hard on yourself. It's not unusual for students to focus on things other than their studies in their first year at university! As you've identified, it's still possible for you to pass your first year (comfortably) and move into the second year, having gained some good life experience and having also learned important lessons about how to engage with your course in the future and, perhaps, choosing who to spend your time with. Those we surround ourselves with have a direct impact on our own behaviour, whether we realise it or not. We are hardwired to mimic the behaviours and attitudes of those around us; so, be very careful about who you let into your inner circle. Yes, I've read the Chimp Paradox. And it is very clear that our chimps want to belong to whoever we are spending time with; so, we mimic and become like those in our social circle. If those in our social circle are not positive, you can imagine the sort of chaos that may ensue, just through our subconscious decisions and actions.

It sounds like you want me to explain a little bit about the types of assessments you're facing. Because I'm coming to the end of my second year now (all still going well for me, thanks), I am a little more familiar with the different means through which assessments occur, and the different typologies of assessments we face at business school. Why different assessments? I asked my lecturer this once. It's partly to keep things interesting for students. It might get repetitive if we only did essays or only did exams, so the diversity is for that reason. It's also so that we can learn to do different sorts of things – write reports, present to other people verbally etc. We will probably need to do these things when we leave university. So, exposure to them now is important. After all, it is a business school, not a business per se.

You mentioned that you have two exams. I don't know if these are multiple choice or essay based, by which I mean the sort of exam where you have to write an answer to an essay question. These exams are just what they are – examinations. You'll have to focus on writing or producing something that gets you as many marks as possible in the allocated time. It's that simple really. I'm assuming you're going to write essays in response to an unseen question. Obviously, have a sense of what sort of things might come up on the paper and an idea of what sort of things you can talk about. It's not unreasonable to ask the module leader to give you some guidance on this, if they've not already. But don't be too rigid! Don't prepare an answer and go to the exam and repeat that answer no matter what, even if that answer is not intrinsically linked to what is asked. The exam is a test of your ability to think and respond to an unseen question, that is think and respond under pressure and in an agile way! (However, if the exam is seen rather than unseen – meaning you know what will be asked a priori and can respond in due course – you can go in with that 'set' attitude). Some people hate exams and get very nervous when doing them. Others like them. On the plus side, they don't take as long to do as an assessment. So, a few hours in an exam hall might be nicer than several hours in a library and at a computer?!

When writing exams, preparation and confidence are everything, I find. If you're someone who gets nervous, breathe properly at the start of the exam (sounds silly I know but it works, and since you seem to be learning about breathing now, you will know the benefits). Realistically, exams are part of life so – like them or not – it's best to get good at doing them. There's an art to passing them and scoring well on them. Learn the strategy of passing. Some students will not have done as well as they would have liked in exams before going to university and will be facing an exam for the first time since school. It is especially important for these students to put the past behind them and focus on the present and the material being assessed now, rather than dwelling on the past or assuming what happened before has to determine what happens now.

You'll be amazed at how confidence dissipates anxiety. Always write a plan before you write an answer in your exam – making sure you reflect on the question that is asked. Spend ten minutes or so on this plan before you write anything and stick to the plan, allowing it to guide you as you write. Don't let the process overwhelm you – take some time to really think about how you can answer the question, plotting the structure of the answer and any key studies or references you can incorporate at certain points; then answer the exam question in relation to this. Of course, the more you know will determine how well you can populate and substantiate your plan. You will have to learn enough – which at business school often means general references to literature as well as case studies. There are all sorts of ways to memorise important information relating to names and dates. The best is visualisation techniques. Instead of trying to remember a name, associate the name with an image in your mind. You'll be amazed how much easier it is to recall information – even in the pressure cooker context of an exam – by doing this technique.

You also have a report. I personally find reports harder to produce than exam answers and essays – which I talk about below. Reports are quite formulaic. This means they are rather uncreative and want you to stick to a template. So, make sure you get a sense of the structure or formula of the report that your lecturers want you to conform to and stick to it. There are some good books on writing reports that are worth looking at. A couple of books to look at might be *Writing a Report* by John Bowden and Reid's *Report Writing*.

Essays – I prefer essays to other forms of assessment, partly as I'm more familiar with them and mainly because I feel they give me a licence to explore areas with some academic freedom and curiosity in a way that other modes of assessment don't permit. It's likely that most of the assessments you will do this year, and in the future, will take an essay format. A good tip I recently got when writing essays is to write the introduction last! It sounds counterintuitive. Obviously, the introduction comes first in terms of the sequence of the essay and what your readers encounter. But as a body of words that you put together, write the introduction last, when you're more familiar with what the essay does and how it contributes. Writing the introduction last allows you to tell the reader what is coming more simply, concisely and accurately. It will ensure a 'fit' between what you say you do and what you do. It will also prompt you to ensure what you claim in the introduction actually correlates to the question being asked. The introduction should navigate the reader.

The main prose – the large body of text after the introduction and before the conclusion – should then answer the question. Using subheadings is often a helpful thing to structure your essay's prose, allowing each section to deal with specific, more detailed aspects of the essay. This can keep the essay clearer, stop convoluted overlap and prevent you from going off on tangents in your discussion. The conclusion then comes and should reflect on the essay; perhaps, suggesting further questions and trajectories. This is a simple structure for essays but will allow you to construct essays that are focused and likely to get you good grades. Why make it more complex than it needs to be? You will then present a bibliography. Further reading on writing essays can be found in Bryan Greetham's book titled *How to Write Better Essays*. If you want to read examples of top-class essays – essays considered classics – you can see *The Oxford Book of Essays*. In there, you will see just how amazing essays can be as a medium of communication. There is an art and science to essay writing.

Presentations are difficult for me as I am quite shy and don't like speaking in front of people. Thankfully, presentations at a business school are normally group based; so, I can get someone else to do the presenting, and I can focus on doing the 'groundwork', organising and researching the information others will present. If there is someone who is naturally a good presenter in your group (maybe that is you?), then let that person present as they will probably enjoy it. Likewise, allow those who naturally enjoy other aspects of putting a presentation together to do what they like to do! Divide labour and let those who are good and enjoy doing certain things do those things. Don't underestimate the non-verbal communication related to presenting: how you use your body and how you use props (e.g. slides and visuals) as well as the words coming out of your mouth are all significant. But present what? It is the responsibility of the team to research what to present and structure the way that information is presented, so the presentation is systematic, logical and – crucially – focused on the assignment brief and set questions.

It's unfortunate that you've not helped the other group members out so far in terms of collectively constructing a presentation, to be brutally honest. That happened to me once, but an inversion of your situation. I was in a group and was doing so much of the work alongside one other member, but two members hardly bothered. They didn't turn up to the meetings we organised, and on the day of the presentation, they stood there like statues. It irritated me. They got the same grade as me! Grades were allocated to the group, not to individuals. So, they benefitted from others' hard work! Is it too late for you to say sorry to the other members, and show them that you are willing to contribute from now on? Perhaps, identifying a particular skill you have, which you can utilise now to help the group obtain a good grade? Putting together slides and visuals, perhaps? For more on presenting well, to get the most you can out of the opportunities to present as a student and receive marks for your presentations, see Nancy Duarte's *Slide: Ology*. This book is interesting as it discusses presenting as both an 'art' and a 'science'. Another good one is Gallo's *Talk Like Ted*. This work helps break down what 'secrets' top public speakers use, so you can emulate them in your own presentations.

Let me say something about writing for assessments more generally. Unless the module is mathematically based or the assessment is multiple choice, how you write is obviously central to getting good grades in the context of assign-ments. Learning to write (and talk) well is such an important skill in life. It opens doors for you. You are useful if you can write and talk clearly and make points that are logical and backed up by evidence. Writing well, as one lecturer said, is not the same as writing in a pompous way, or making things more complicated than they need to be! Using unnecessarily complex words and sentences is often something people do to disguise the fact that, below the pompous writing, there is no real substance. People who write this way are often trying to impress others, but the only people who are impressed by shallow, 'posh' sounding writing are those who don't see through it. If you strip complex words – or even worse, pretentious academic jargon – back, it's possible that all that is left is platitudes or waffle. Beware of this! Instead, write simply and clearly, and read work that follows these principles. The more you write, the better at it you will become. It's an art. So, keep practising. See these end-of-year assessments not as a burden but as chances to practice and hone your writing skills, by which I mean writing in a structured way and in relation to set questions while using taught materials. This is meaningful practice for your writing. There are detailed books on writing that you might look at. A classic one, which a lecturer suggested to me and which I enjoyed, is William Zinsser's book On Writing Well.

Your question on analysis is harder to answer. As my second year has evolved, I have learned that there is a fundamental difference between presenting work that 'describes' and work that 'analyses'. For you to do well, you must start producing work that complies with the latter not the former. The simplest way of making this difference between analysis and description clear is by stepping back and thinking of two related questions when you read what you've read: 'so what?' and 'how does this answer the question'?

A descriptive essay tells a story. It might even use taught material and wider reading to tell that story. But the story does not really get to the root of what is being asked. It may be a collection of information – albeit apparently relevant information – jumbled together, but the information fails to be applied to what is being asked. Or the information chosen to 'evidence' the story might be so basic that it stops you – as a writer – using that information to demonstrate the sort of understanding needed to elicit good grades. This often happens when students decide to not use the suggested reading to analyse and, instead, find their own sources. So, it will be hard for a descriptive essay to get into the 60s (a 2:1). Your lecturers might provide a **marking grid** with your essays to help you understand what they are attributing marks for. Without analysis, it will be hard to achieve almost any dimension of a properly thought-out marking grid.

An analytical essay also tells a story – using taught material, wider reading and possible other things like statistics and visuals. In this regard, a descriptive and analytical essay may seem quite similar on the surface. But dig deeper, and there are differences, and these differences will matter significantly to those assessing you. The analytical essay answers the set question directly. The assessor does not read sections of the essay and think 'so what?' and 'how does this answer the question'. Instead, an analytical essay is using material purposefully to craft an answer. The more nuanced, deep and sophisticated the analysis, the better the grade will be. Analytical discussions are not presented in a random way or loosely related to what is being asked. Analytical work directly takes on what is being asked; there is not a sense of 'so what?' Rather each paragraph is doing something explicit and beneficial in terms of getting grades and analysing materials to come to that grade.

Different perspectives might be presented in the analytical essay, showing readers that the student has understood different – maybe contrasting – viewpoints on the topic, to give an objective insight, analysing the way these perspectives help understand the topic and, perhaps, the strengths and weaknesses of these views. For example – to use two different perspectives that I was introduced to today which are fresh in my mind – the analytical essay might analyse a question from a Managerial Perspective and a Critical Perspective. The former is rooted in looking at things from the view of the manager (not the workers) and is focused on making money. The latter is more concerned with the workers (not the manager) and has its roots in Marxism. It is aware of exploitation – perceived or real – rather than making money per se. These perspectives offer different views on the same thing. How you run a business and treat people in that business will be very different depending on which view you follow. By engaging with these views in the analytical essay, a richer response can be presented. Analytical discussions are not 'black and white'; instead, analysis is measured to show the student has understood shades of grey in their analysis. The story – or analysis – follows a logical trajectory and pattern, finding a flow and argument.

It's hard to know the difference between description and analysis when you first start thinking about essays properly, by which I mean in a way where you think about how to craft essays that will get grades and where you, as a writer, are more conscious of what a good essay constitutes. I find writing essays, drafting, redrafting and redrafting again is the best way to start understanding how these differences evolve from abstract ideas to realities that your writing is aware of and expresses. Read your work as if you're assessing it – thinking, if I was grading this, would I be attributing marks to it? Which sections are stronger and clearer, and which are weaker? How does this whole essay fit together as a series of smaller components? In this way, see the essay through the eyes of your lecturer, without the lecturer being there. Remember to order the argument in clear paragraphs, with each paragraph having a purpose and each paragraph contributing to the wider essay. Analytical writing becomes – eventually – tacit knowledge; a sort of second nature or instinct. As does locating analytical writing within a proper structure. Planning the essay (which bits go where) and using subheadings to help order the essay can't be overestimated as acts to engage in when producing analytical work. The more you do it, the more you start to write analytically.

As I've said before, when analysing, write simply and concisely. Be precise with the words you use. Words are powerful and will 'package' the analysis. The essays that I've got high grades for have always been simply presented but really purposeful in using the material to analyse and bolster my arguments. Often, universities have 'study skills centres' – or places like that – where the foundations of writing and studying are taught. I hear, anecdotally, different things about these: some universities seem to have very helpful study skills events and teachers. Others, less so. Perhaps, see what is available to you?

One of my lecturers recently recommended a book to me which I wish I had read when I started university. The book does a really good job of articulating many of the things I knew to be true, intuitively, in terms of presenting work that is logical, rational and substantive but which I couldn't quite articulate in my mind and use to inform my assessments. It is – in my lecturers' words – 'an oldie but a goodie'. That book is Alec Fisher's *The Logic of Real Arguments*. The work helps you analyse, evaluate and construct your own arguments. This book is really helpful to you as a student doing assignments as it will help you construct logical, real arguments within your assignments.

For example, a question Fisher asks via the book is 'What argument or evidence would justify me in believing P?'. Let's evolve this to your question. If you're presenting p in an assignment and saying P is the basis of your answer, you better make sure that P is well argued, and that you convince readers why you (and they) should believe in P. You can't expect a good mark if your arguments are weak and lacking logic. There could be views other than and counter to P. Have these been discussed? Have you shown how and why P is better? Have you shown how P can be understood more fully by considering A, B, C and other views?

You're still asking about bibliographies. I'm almost at the end of my second year and I still have course-mates confused about them. They are quite simple really. There are different referencing styles (at my business school we use the Harvard system, but I have friends at other business schools who use British standards) and the referencing style the business school requires will determine the bibliography you produce. There are some really good external references to look at, which explain citations in much more detail than I can. I looked at these in the first year and it was time well spent, as I've been able to craft bibliographies quite easily and simply ever since. The best I found is here: https://www.citethemrightonline.com/

This is the 'citethemright' website. It is the Bible on citing! It's an online resource which derives from and compliments the book by the same name, written by Richard Pears and Graham Shields, which is now on its 12th edition. There is a standard way to reference and it's important you learn these standards and demonstrate them in your assessed work.

More generally, I wonder: have you engaged with your lecturers when preparing work? Lecturers are very happy to help students prepare work – though there are conditions attached to this, which I'll come to. If there are 'workshops' built into the module, you really should attend them as they are a chance to work on the assessment via a closer relationship with the lecturer who might guide you on what to do (and why to do). While lecturers won't look at drafts of work, they can look at plans – at least at my business school. If you can't attend workshops, you can always email lecturers with specific questions or see them after a lecture. Ask precise, specific questions. They are busy people but are often passionate and want to help their students do well. When I say 'conditions', I mean to emphasise that there is a certain sort of relationship between a lecturer (especially one who is going to mark your work and one who has spent many years learning about and researching a topic) and a student. Don't be defensive: if the lecturer gives you honest advice and feedback, remember it's not personal or an insight into how they judge you morally! It's just them doing their job, trying to help you prepare for work. Don't assume or come across like you think you know more than the lecturer. Arrogance is not a good basis for any relationship, Also – because they are busy and factual – they might answer your email questions very directly. Don't mistake this for something it is not – it is probably the most professional and succinct way for them to answer your questions. Lecturers are there to help guide you, but not collaborate with you! The worst thing you can do is email or approach a lecturer with a sense of entitlement along the lines of 'I know best' and/or 'because I am paying fees, I expect x from you'. It says more about the student than the lecturer when students approach academics with this sort of mentality: do you really think such an approach is the best one to get what you want, that is detailed feedback and suggestions on how to elevate your work? It's sort of a negotiation process you're entering, so give the lecturer reasons to want to help you (the best reason being this student is honestly trying to learn and wants to do well). I have seen a number of students get themselves into trouble for approaching lecturers with a sense of entitlement and the implication that their 'feelings' are what's important here, rather than a learning journey.

Another book I recently came across through a module leader – and this is a book you might not expect to read at a business school – is called *Can't Hurt Me: Master Your Mind and Defy the Odds*. The book is written by David Goggins – a remarkable man who is a former elite US Navy seal and holder of various records linked to physical strength and endurance. The book is about how to reach our full potential in life and the extent to which doing so is a mental game. He challenges readers to 'callous their minds': become mentally tough and resilient, drop your ego and watch your life change as you get out of your comfort zone. Embrace the toughness and challenges, realising they strengthen you and give you resilience. I loved it. I suggest reading it as it'll help build a mental toughness that will be so valuable to you as a student, at work and in life in general; especially at a time when mental toughness – though such a great commodity and resource – is in such short supply.

I've just suggested a book that will tell you to be disciplined and focused and build structure and routine. So, this may sound contradictory. But before I finish the email, I want to make a wider point about year one. You have to ask what is the point of year one? Year one is a transition phase. In that sense, it's not a disaster that you're at this point – a sort of mini crisis based on a very real prospect that you may fail the first year. The grades you get in year one will not impact your final degree classification. The main point is to develop the skills you need in years two and three. You will keep learning and honing skills in years two and three. Your degree is designed to get harder incrementally and keep testing – but also refining – your skills. In another sense, year one is unique. You might never get an opportunity to enjoy yourself as much again! I'm an introvert and my idea of enjoyment is not partying. But if yours is, so be it. Maybe those hedonistic urges are out of your system, and you can focus on work more in year two, having learned important lessons both inside and outside the lecture hall. Try and get a balance between fun and work in year two. Where the balance is? That's for you to decide.

Eve

Part Two: Lifestyle Choices

Adam also sent an email to Titus. His email to Titus was a little more honest and direct in terms of revealing how hopeless he felt and how much he regrets not focusing more.

From: Adam
To: Titus
Subject: Help, I'm going to fail the first year (and sorry).

Hi Titus, Adam here. First, let me say sorry. You took so much time to give me all that really helpful and clear advice in our last email exchange. Since we last spoke, there has been times when I've managed to act on some of the lessons and suggestions. When I have, I have felt well and had a sense of progress. But in truth, I wasn't disciplined enough to follow your suggestions with any real consistency. I did the opposite. Sorry! I have not slept well – I've been out far too much. The only consistent thing about my sleeping patterns is going to bed late, getting up late and often waking up panicking about work, money and other things. I have not eaten well; I've hardly exercised and the closest I got to an ice bath was when I fell in a river one evening. I spend more time on social media than doing pretty much anything else. My life feels like its spiralling and my work has suffered dramatically. I am in debt and have no real idea how to start all the assessments. But I keep doing the same things despite this – out with 'friends', night after night; worrying all day, then out again, or having lots of people over in our hall. Hoping this next night out will do the trick and somehow solve all my problems. Or convincing myself that tomorrow it will all change, but of course it doesn't. Sometimes it's as if I'm observing myself from the outside, on this destructive and unproductive journey, knowing I could do things to stop this cycle. But it's like there's part of me choosing not to stop it; instead going further and further into it. I also emailed my friend Eve to get her advice on what to do. Although I didn't outline, so honestly to her, where I am or why am I here.

I did read the *Chimp Paradox* – what a book. It's one of the few things I have read this year, though I really enjoyed it. Sadly, my chimp is in control, seeking pleasure in the form of immediate gratification and not implementing a long-term strategy for success. It's not even like I've really enjoyed this cycle I'm in – it just leads to depression and a sense of meaninglessness. I didn't join any clubs. I'm just spending time with others who are all on the verge of failing their first year and who also seem to have destructive tendencies. Thinking back to your last message: I don't think I even like these people who I am around. I am sure they will not be there for me if I need them but helping me required them to sacrifice anything. I am not myself around them. I feel forced to put on a version of me. I don't think these people want the best for me. I'm probably naive and not a great judge of character.

Why does this matter? What am I actually messaging you about? I need advice because I have six modules that all have assignments due soon. I 'only' need 40% to pass the first year and proceed to year 2. But at the moment, I don't think I'll get that. My friend Eve, whom I told you about in another email, has given me a detailed pathway forward academically. In addition to the suggestions that you made in your last email – which I really should read again and try to implement in terms of living a lifestyle that enables me to progress – do you have anything else for me? Something short term and quick, to get me walking in a new direction? A quick win that might change my momentum.

I am going to attack these assignments and I'm going to pull my socks off. I promise. My future depends on it. Otherwise, it's my first year again (another year of studying, another year of debt) or I'll have to come home and somehow find a job in a very depressed labour market – the sort of job I never wanted in the first place and the avoidance of which was a motivation for me coming to university in the first place.

Adam

In response, Titus sent the following email.

From: Titus
To: Adam
Subject: RE: Help, I'm going to fail the first year (and sorry).

Adam, you need to 'disappear'. What that means is to come off social media, stop going out, perhaps turn your phone off so nobody can contact you (except for family) for extended periods of time and go under the radar. Give yourself space and time to breathe and produce and recover. And just focus on work. Get this work done. Cultivate the suggestions I made in the last email as a framework to live in while you hide. You can reappear. But when you do, reappear as someone who has passed the first year and as someone you and others can respect. If needs be, see this as a temporary but necessary escape. The life you describe and the 'friends' you mention will be there when you reappear, if you choose to go back to it. You have a small window to save a key time in your life. It's hard to emphasise how integral this period of time – passing the first year – is to your whole future, not just at university but afterwards. Think of kids you might have in the future, think of a partner not yet met. Think of what you'd say to yourself now in your 40s or 50s about the opportunities that might come your way if only you can – frankly – grow up a bit and move forward. It's the first year! It's not that hard to pass. The rewards for passing are multiple. The penalties for failing may be catastrophic. You don't need to go to an extreme and start studying for 12 hours a day. You just need to move forward, find a routine and focus on the goal – passing first year, and moving on as a better version of who you are now and who has learned from past mistakes.

What is the point of the first year? Let's put it into context. If we reduce it down to purely academics – so ignoring all the wider lessons outside of university – you just have to pass. You just have to do enough to go on to the second year. There is this real versus imagined thing with the first year. Some imagine it to be such a more demanding process than what came before it, at school. For most courses at most universities, this is not the case. The semesters, and your degree over the years, should get incrementally more demanding. You just have to keep up. If you want to stretch and challenge yourself, as high-achieving students do, there should be scope in your degree for this to happen. But for most, passing is enough.

Then there is this almost cliched view of how to 'have fun' and 'be a fresher', which is partying to excess. If that floats your boat, fair play. But there has to be a balance. Realise this. Implement this balance. I bet that if you were to access all the lecture slides and lecture recordings that have happened and listen to them, you'll be able to get a sense of what has been taught, why it has been taught and how to engage with it in your assessments. Doing this is a small investment in time relatively, but hugely productive. Maybe this is the easy win or quick fix you seek, to change momentum? That's all I did for my first year.

In my first year, I also was out a lot (still am): playing rugby four times a week and socialising. But I also made sure that I found a balance. And in those periods, when it matters – that is, during business time – I found that a lot of what I needed to know was there and accessible. For a while, I just wasn't looking in the right places or listening to the right people. But once I navigated the system – once I got institutional knowledge specific to my business school and degree – I began to organise myself and my thoughts. I'm not particularly academic or a hard worker. I am a typical, average, middle-of-the-road student. But that's enough, so long as you do enough consistently.

You can get out of this situation and slump. When the going gets tough, the tough get going. Believe in yourself. Learn to be mentally tough and resilient. Dig in. Have a sense of perspective. You're very fortunate in a grand scheme of things. Let's not have a pity party.

Sorry to be so harsh! But sometimes harshness and truth are the kindest teachers.

From your friend,

Titus

Summary of Key Points

- There are different modes of assessment at university.
- These modes of assessment require and test different sorts of skills.
- Analysis is an important concept and your work should 'analyse' as deeply as possible. The ability to analyse is perhaps the most important skill required at the level of assessment at university.
- How you react to adversity is a key part of life, and surviving business school and what comes after it. Adversity can include not getting the grades you want or finding yourself, through your own decisions and actions, in a situation that appears problematic and challenging.

Things to Think About

- How might you best prepare for the different types of assessments that will come your way at business school?
- How do 'analysis' and 'description' differ?
- What is a bibliography?
- What are the advantages of discussing your assessment(s) with your lecturer(s) before you submit your assignment?

Exercises/Questions for Discussion

- What mode of assessment is most suited to you and your learning style? Why?
- What three things can you do in order to improve your assessment performance?

- How can you build 'analysis' into your assessments? How can you be sure your assessments display a level of analysis?
- Do you react well when things – like the grades you get – don't go the way you want and hope? How can you learn from past reactions to improve how you react in the future?

Glossary Terms

Bibliography: a list of references, presented at the end of your assessment, to show readers (i.e. those marking your work) which references you have used to substantiate your work.

Essay: the most common form of assessment at university; a body of text that allows students to discuss concepts and themes in order to address a set question.

Exams: normally an unseen question or set of questions that students answer in a specified set of time. In the past, exams occurred in exam halls. More recently, exams have been answered online, with students addressing set questions from their homes. This type of exam became popular during the COVID lockdowns.

Feedback: those marking your work should explain why you got the grade you got and, ideally, how you can get higher grades in the future. This explanation represents 'feedback'. Feedback will normally be sent to you electronically in written form when your assignment is returned. However, feedback can also be verbal. Students often focus more on the grade they get than the feedback with their grade; but good feedback is invaluable in terms of learning from the past.

Marking grid: a rubric, normally communicated to students, which specifies what those marking an assessment take into account when giving that assessment a grade. The more an assessment complies with the requirements of a marking grid the better, in general, that assessment will do.

Pass and proceed: a decision conferred by the board of examiners on the students at the end of their first and second years, allowing them to enter the next stage of their degree, having shown suitable performance.

Presentation: a chance for students to stand up and discuss what they know or have found out about a topic which they have been asked to investigate. Often, presentations are constructed by a group of students.

Report: a form of assessment that is formulaic and often formal in its tone. Reports are means of communicating which are often used and expected in 'the world of business'.

Resit: the chance for a student to 'resit' – that is retake – an assessment that they have failed. Pass and proceed may be conferred on a student subject to them passing a resit.

Further Reading

Bowden, J. (2011). Writing a Report. How to books.

Duarte, N. (2008). Slide:ology: the art and science of creating great presentations. O'Reilly Media.

Fisher A. (2004). The Logic of Real Arguments. Cambridge University Press.

Gallo, C. (2014). Talk Like Ted: the 9 public speaking secrets of the world's top minds. St. Martin's Press.

Goggins, D. (2018). Can't Hurt Me: Master Your Mind and Defy the Odds. Lioncrest Publishing.

Greetham, B. (2018). How to write better essays. Macmillan study skills.

Pears, R and Shields, G. (2022). Cite Them Right: The Essential Referencing Guide. Bloomsbury Study Skills.

Reid, M. (2012). Report Writing. Palgrave.

Zinsser, W. (2006). On Writing Well. Turtleback books.

4

EMPLOYMENT AND EMPLOYABILITY

Part One: Thinking about Employability

Adam passed his first year. He has returned to business school, feeling enthusiastic and relieved, as he starts the first semester of his second year. He sends an email to Titus. His thoughts are turning to employment, as well as business school. Here is an email he sends.

From: Adam
To: Titus
Subject: A fresh start

Hi there, how are you?

Well, I passed my first year in the end. What a relief! Things were getting a little scary for a while. I read my email back to myself – the one I sent to you. It sounds like a different person wrote that now. It's funny how time can change one's perspective, mood and outlook.

I'm now in my second year, a few weeks in. I am implementing a number of your life lessons in my own life, and I am much happier in general for doing so. I am living a more focused, productive life. I'm back in the gym and even thinking about playing some rugby again. I certainly have a better balance now than what I did have. I've also got rid of as many negative influences in my life as I could – certain people, certain habits and certain modes of thinking I'd

---

DOI: 10.4324/9781003467397-5

developed, which were habitual but holding me back. I realised I lacked confidence and wanted to fit in. A lot of the sort of self-sabotaging behaviour I was participating in was an attempt to get validation. I was letting others pull my strings, a puppet dancing to other people's tunes. I was not in control of my life directly, making my own decisions.

Academically, when I started engaging with the course material (you were right – it was all there – in slides and recordings), I realised how much I like what I am studying. I realised how well organised that material is and how I could quite easily dive into it and reproduce it in ways that would allow me to pass assessments. I have managed to keep that momentum so far, going into my second year.

Enough of me. What about you? You'll be in your third year now? Same as Eve. I'm thinking about applying for a job while I study. I'll be sure to save some money if I do, as you suggested some time ago. Some people on my course are talking about applying for a placement year. Do you know anything about this?

Thanks again for all your support. You were right – I needed to grow up and disappear.

Adam

Titus replies to Adam, through the following message.

From: Titus
To: Adam
Subject: RE: A fresh start

Hi Adam,
I am delighted to hear that you've made those changes in your life. I think you will be amazed at how much better your life will be – in the short and long term – if you continue to follow the trajectory you are on. Remember, we only need a 1% improvement daily, but we do want that improvement daily. One thing I believe is that it's very important to be the master of your own ship. This means making your own decisions and forming your own path, instead of conforming to other people's expectations. When you are brave enough to do this and embrace the freedom that comes with it, then your life really starts. Otherwise, you're essentially an actor: acting how you think others want. This is duplicitous, to you and others. It might be

well-meaning to comply and please, but it's an abysmal long-term strategy. Remember, this is a journey. You will make mistakes. Don't worry if and when you do make mistakes. Just go back to being kind to yourself, and implementing the rules again, one day at a time. It's consistency you want, over time. Not sudden, dramatic changes that are likely to fail the test of time and are little more than hype.

Jobs generally are a great idea. So, I'm happy to hear that you're thinking about getting one. It's great to have an income and save as much as you can! But are you sure a job is what you need now? It sounds like you're starting to get into a mode of living and thinking that you need to achieve long-term goals. While there are lots of positivises associated with working, you don't want to take on too much and lose any momentum you've built up. Working requires time and energy. These are finite resources. Do you have enough of them to expend right now? All success in life requires sacrifice in the short term: the athlete lives a certain life now and forgoes certain pleasures now to perform later. Same for us. Don't worry about foregoing work (and pay) now if it means better work and options in the future. Don't get me wrong – if you can combine both, that's great. And in the future having actual 'work experience' that you can talk about and evidence will be potentially vital to securing post-university employment. But for you as an individual right now, is it the best option?

You're right – I would be in my third year! But I'm not. No – I've not left university! Instead, I took advantage of an opportunity that came my way: an opportunity to spend a year in industry. So, I will still spend three years at business school studying, but between years two and three of studying I will be working. So, suddenly my three-year degree became a four-year degree, with one year working in industry. Some people call this a **placement year** or a **sandwich year**. This is an option most business school degrees offer. The benefits of working in a structured environment like this – in addition to studying as part of your degree – are multiple. Perhaps, the best benefit I've realised so far is linked to practically doing and learning.

You can read lots of books about how to do management (or marketing, or entrepreneurship or whatever else you're studying) but until you're applying this knowledge in a proper setting – with real people and with real deadlines and in relation to real problems and objectives and setbacks – what you've read is always just abstract. When you work, the knowledge becomes alive and relevant. You realise how little you know. You may have knowledge in terms of knowing what books and journal articles say, but can you convert that knowledge into doing? I've made a large number of mistakes already (thankfully those supervising me spotted the mistakes and either remedied them or gave me the chance to remedy them). This is all humiliating. But if we are being open to learning and showing humility, then failing is the foundation of meaningful learning. A surgeon must learn to do surgery, going from reading about it to doing it. As part of this, mistakes will be made (that's how they learn) and the more experienced surgeons might have to step in at times. It's a dramatic example, and when mistakes are made in the surgery room they are, of course, more important and significant than the ones we make! But it's the same in business. We must learn to do. Sometimes we need help and guidance from more experienced hands, as they point out and fix our errors. Working here has shown me this and helped me live these principles. I have been pleasantly surprised by how much I am enjoying working. I guess I am a 'routine person' – I benefit from doing the same things most days. Like the summer when I worked on the building site, what I have now is a solid routine. But it is certainly more stressful and tiring than being a student.

I'm spending structured time in different divisions of the firm I'm spending my placement year in (marketing, finance, HR and the call centre talking to clients – all over). So, I am getting exposed to a wide range of experiences. I am learning the day-to-day technical skills required to do the job. Once learned, the skills are ingrained and you just repeat them. In a way it's repetitive. I guess the world of work is about learning processes and procedures and doing and repeating them over and over again. In another way, it's about learning to be consistent and concentrate. There are also all sorts of '**soft skills**' I wasn't aware of which are really important in the workplace and which I don't think should be underestimated but which are not really taught to us, certainly not at school or business schools. Here I'm talking about things like knowing how to tie a tie properly and knowing how to talk to clients (listening more than talking – so you can understand what they need and deliver it). These might sound intuitive, but it's amazing how important they are in the world of work, and it might be the case that you don't actually have the level of soft skills you think you have. I certainly don't.

Anyway, I'm just a few weeks into the placement. I'll tell you more about it in the future when I've been here longer and maybe have more experience to draw on. Often, a well-structured placement will give you exposure to several aspects of the business in the first six to eight months, then see you specialise in the latter parts of the placement, focusing more specifically and intensely on one area. Perhaps, I will draw on these experiences in the future when I may be able to talk more candidly and knowledgeably.

Keep working hard. Take care, Adam.

Titus

Adam also emails Eve to get more details and advice about employment and employability. Here is an email he sent to Eve.

From: Adam
To: Eve
Subject: Work
Date: year two, semester 1

Hi Eve. I was really quite stressed when I last emailed. You might remember that I was struggling as my first year came to an end. Anyway, I managed to sort myself out. I passed the year with a high 2:2, averaging around 57%. So, I'm now in my second year, about four weeks in. Thanks for the advice. It helped loads. I am determined to be more organised this year, giving myself time to plan work, read and edit assessments before submitting, making sure I (try to) analyse properly and write clearly and – most of all – answer questions. I am determined to get a 2:1 or maybe a first this year and next year.

Just as I feel like I'm starting to get to grips with the academic aspects of being at business school, a new set of questions arise, around employment. I am starting to think about getting a job while I study. Partly because I'd like to have more money and partly because I think it will be good for me. This job will be your 'typical' student job, like working in a bar or pub or coffee shop; something to do alongside my studies. I'm also thinking about trying to get some work experience in the sort of organisation I might like to work in when I leave. (I always wanted to have my own business, but I'm starting to think working for someone else for a while might be a better short-term plan). By this I mean a sort of office-based, 9–5 job, working with my brain in the 'knowledge economy', in a graduate job where they require a degree. As part of my degree, I have the option to study for three years (which means I'm almost at the halfway point – scary) or do a four-year degree. The four-year degree still means three years of studying but also a placement year, where I could work for a firm for a year before coming back and completing my finals. In the past, students on my course have spent a year working for major, multinational firms (as well as more local firms). What do you think of that?

I want to be a person who does more and does more better – in terms of work, realising my economic potential and ensuring I treat others and myself properly. All sorts. Maybe I'm growing up. Maybe it's a phase.

Anyway, I better get on with reading, and also filling in some job applications, to work as a part-time barista at a local coffee shop. I heard that you'd been applying for jobs – like proper career jobs – so that you have work ready for you when you graduate. It was your Mum who told me this when I bumped into her over the summer. She is very proud of you. It was clear how pleased she is with who you are. This should not be underestimated.

Have a nice day. Hope to hear from you soon.

Adam

Eve replies through the below. Eve is in an excellent position to respond to Adam because of recent experiences she has had, which have culminated in Eve receiving significant job offers.

From: Eve
To: Adam
Subject: RE: Work

Hello again. I am delighted to hear that you passed your first year. Keep up the diligent approach to studying! I'm pleased you liked the suggested reading, too!

In terms of getting a part-time job while you're studying: yes, that's a good idea. First, you can make some money, as you said. Second, you will learn important life skills. This will all help when you leave university, whether that's when being interviewed for jobs, in jobs or developing your own business. For example, by doing part-time work now, you will learn to deal with people. That is a great skill. It is hard to deal with other people, such as co-workers and – especially – the general public. Prospective employers will be impressed that you can do this: looking people in the eye, communicating, listening and resolving problems or providing a good service. Also, you will learn to turn up on time, even when you don't want to. So, by working now, you will learn discipline and time management. This is good for you and signals to others that you're employable and trustworthy. You might have to do jobs you don't want to (cleaning toilets!) or learn new skills on the job. Again, this is all good for you. And it signals to others that you have humility and a willingness to learn and that you don't assume you're too good to do the hard jobs in life.

The only caveat: working part-time is a great idea so long as it doesn't get in the way of you spending time on your university work! Time and energy are at a premium, so make sure you can combine the two worlds of paid work and university work! If not, forgo the job. You have the rest of your life to work. You only have this small window – which, as you say, is almost halfway done – to get that 2:1 or a first. (Time really does fly – they told me this when I started – it's only now, in my final year, that I appreciate this).

The other option you have, of course, is making some money while you study as a sole trader. This means thinking of a business idea (a service or product) and registering as a sole trader and making money that way. This is a very underrated and underexplored option that students have, but often ignore. Not very entrepreneurial! Some people I have studied with have done very well for themselves financially by designing and selling t-shirts, for example, and even making their own events and marketing businesses. They promote university events or other social events in the city and get paid to do this, having fun too. (There's more to life than 'being an influencer': a short-term and vapid aspiration if ever there was one – what seems like an easy, short-term solution almost never is). They will probably continue doing this work when they leave university. If you're serious about having your own business and being your own boss, what better time to dip your toe in the water, so to speak than now? There is little risk in starting a business, so if it fails the consequences are small. If it takes off, though, you may have laid the foundations of a business empire that stands the test of time! Applying all that entrepreneurial knowledge you've paid to learn, and using that knowledge to make money, sounds like a good option for you. Also, this option means you're your own boss, so you can decide when to work and how much work to do, around the more important task of performing well academically in your second year.

If you get the chance to do a placement year, I really think you should. My business school also offers this. A lecturer told me how much more mature students are when they come back having had a 'year out'. He even said that statistics show that students who do a placement year are considerably more likely to get a first. This could be that better students get placements, so better students would have got a first without a placement, of course. But there are other variables to consider this correlation in relation to: by a placement year, students learn a work ethic and particular mindset from working, where they are perhaps more confident and more able to manage their time and deadlines and produce work that is more 'grounded'. Another advantage is opportunities are offered to students who have done a year in industry. Their experience is invaluable and sets them apart from the multitude of other applicants applying for graduate jobs, or 'graduate schemes' as they are known, once they complete their degree. Also, if you do well in the placement year, it's often the case that the firm will recruit you in the future. So, it's a win–win.

Be aware though that placements are highly competitive. Lots of people will apply for a small number of places. These people will be from your business school and business schools all over the country. That said, I know people in the year above who got placements at major firms in major cities, in the UK and internationally. I didn't apply for a placement in my second year – if I had and was successful, I'd be doing work now, rather than doing what I'm doing – my third and final year. I am enjoying year three but also looking forward to the end of university.

In a way, I'm pleased to be 'just' studying my final year, rather than studying my final year *and* applying for jobs. (Please note here that I'm talking about jobs below – full-time, permanent jobs after I graduate. This is different to a placement year, working for a year as part of my degree). I've been applying for jobs intensely. I started in the summer and have been working on applications since. The good news is that I've ended up with four job offers. I have firmly accepted one, which I will start almost as soon as I finish my degree, so long as I get a 2:1.

It might sound like because I've been offered four – not just one job – in the current economy and climate that my application was somehow unique or that there is some sort of secret that I mastered in the application process. The truth is job applications are a numbers game. I applied for so many jobs. My other friends who applied for a lot of jobs (and we are talking dozens here) also got jobs or got close to job offers. Those who 'only' applied for a small number didn't.

Two of the job offers I received are with really big, multinational firms. The jobs are specifically designed for graduates – like we will be soon. They are an entry point into a well-known, cohesive firm, so graduates can go in and learn to do specific things, in a structured environment. Over time, these graduates will work their way up in the firm, assuming they stay with them. If they move to another firm, the fact they have 'spent time' with a prestigious firm is a good thing as it signals to others that they are competent – or at least competent enough to enter and maintain a role in a demanding culture.

If you're applying for similar roles in the future, I strongly suggest that you don't leave applications to the last minute. They have deadlines on them, and a rushed application will read like a rushed application. This obviously won't give the prospective employer the message that you're serious, grownup and organised. If you want a 'graduate' job to start shortly after completing your degree, you must be organised and start applying early. Also, to reiterate what I said before: this is a numbers game – the more things you apply for, the better chance you have of getting an interview. Also, don't rehash or 'copy and paste' applications. Write applications that are specific to the firm and job you're applying for. My application was strong – I have academic prizes; I'm predicted to get a first and I had strong references. But, still, I got many rejections. That said, I did get interviews with four firms and, latterly, offers from these four firms.

You want a graduate job but don't want to apply in the standard way? The only other 'routes' into graduate jobs that I see occurring – and the first is very rare – are as follows. Firstly, nepotism! If someone's family is really well connected, they might be able to land a job on that basis. If this seems unjust, it's because it is. I know one friend who is so talented academically and multilingual and has so much to offer but who didn't get a job at a particular firm. Instead, another person we know got it. That person is lazy. But they have connections. Like it or not, this is how the world works – or can work, sometimes. The only solace is that, in the world of work, connections will not cut it; and that firm has lost a genuinely good candidate to a rival. The second – fairer – route to access in a way that bypasses the normal application process and bureaucracy is by doing a *placement year* with a firm as part of your degree, like I talked about above; then drawing on that placement year to gain employment after graduating with the firm you spent time with. This way, you know what you're going into – the everyday reality of that firm and its culture – and the firm knows what they're getting. It's like a 'trial period' or extended probation period. This is not an option for you as you're not doing a placement. But others should be aware of it. Treat every day during the placement as a chance to showcase your abilities, then in the future that hard work might pay off in the form of a job offer and those in power having a favourable view of your application.

The job offers I received came through processes that followed almost identical structures or processes. I will outline them here in case it helps you get your head around what access to a graduate firm looks like in terms of milestones. You search for available jobs. This is an online search. It's probably best to search within specific industries. Available jobs will be clustered on an industry basis, for example in banking, in marketing, in consultancy etc. By jobs I'm talking here about 'graduate jobs'; so, these are jobs where you will enter and be taught industry-specific skills and where a degree is normally required. These are normally well-paid jobs with really good benefits (like pension schemes and holidays). By well paid, I mean well paid in relation to the national average wage, which is lower than a lot of graduates appreciate. It's unlikely that you will enter a firm and immediately be making the sort of eye-watering salary some on my course seem to expect and feel entitled to. You have to prove your worth over time. The top roles are limited and other graduates with lots of experience will be going for those. Walk before you run! The sorts of jobs I'm talking about here are general and range from private firms in cities to roles in the public sector, like with the police force and army. Once in a firm, there is the chance to progress – in terms of salary and status – quite quickly.

Remember that a very large amount of people are applying for a small number of opportunities in these firms. Also, these firms recruit less at the moment than in the past – the economy is not as strong; so, taking on more employees is not a given. Will they even read your application? You have to trust they will. Therefore, how do you make your application stand out and give yourself the best chance of proceeding to the next stage of the application process? There are ways, and I was amazed by how much help the career service at my university gave me. I have friends at other universities who also benefitted greatly from engaging with their career services. Help ranges from putting a CV together to participating in 'mock' or practice interviews and helping you polish and hone your performance on the big day. The more help you can get, the better. If you know someone 'on the inside' – that is, already at a firm – who is able to review and critique your application before you submit it and give you feedback to help, then that might turn out to be golden for you and dramatically increase the strength of your application.

If you manage to get an interview, you can assume that your **application** and **CV** suggest to those evaluating it that you have something – or more likely a number of things – that make them interested in you. Which means, they're interested in the idea that you're someone who they can take on and mould into being what they want and need you to be, as a (paid) resource in their organisation. At the most pragmatic – even cynical – level, that is what is happening: they're looking for cogs to work in their machine. In return, they will pay you. So, if we reduce the interview down to its most functional and pragmatic basis, you must see the interview as a test: is this person someone that can work here, that can 'fit in' here? Will they annoy existing staff and clients? Or will they adhere to the organisational culture? Can they deliver under pressure? Are they keen and enthusiastic? Are they serious, grownup applicants?

Of course, different firms want and are looking for different things in applicants. (Someone in a very client-facing role, for example, who is generating sales might have to show different, more 'bubbly' and extraverted personality than someone doing IT programming, who rarely interacts with clients and whose introversion and immersion in work and numbers rather than people may be perceived as a strength in that context). So, put on your 'best face' in the interview. But don't pretend to be someone you're not! If they reject you, you want them to reject you rather than a version of you which you contrived. Also, if they hire you, you want to know you can be yourself (as you were in the interview) rather than put on an act and pretence and having to extend the performance in the interview into working life. Essentially, such acting – though well intentioned – is a form of deception.

Of course, they will be interviewing other people, with similar if not better attributes than you. So, take the interview seriously. If you can read around the firm you're interviewing at and show in the interview that you're interested and aware of them, that is a strength. Think about how you can contribute to the firm as it is now, specifically, knowing its place in the market and the challenges it faces. As well as what you say verbally, be aware of what you're saying non-verbally in the interview. Use strong, confident and open body language. Listen carefully to what is being asked and answer what is being asked directly. Take a breath before answering and think about your answer. Also, think about your appearance. First appearances matter, as they say. Again, there are different rules and norms around appearances in different industries and contexts: some tech startup which sees itself as 'hip' might expect you to dress one way – perhaps with a quirky haircut, even piercings and tattoos – while a bank, for example, might expect a much more formal appearance and style: pinstripe suits and a crisp white shirt. Conform to what is expected. The phrase 'when in Rome' springs to mind.

In my experience, if the interview goes well (meaning they see you as a good fit for the firm and someone who can make a contribution), they will then ask you back to participate in aptitude tests. Now this is certainly not the case for all, perhaps most, firms. Most of my friends got offers (or rejections) after interviews and did not have to participate in aptitude tests. But for the firms I applied to, I had to do aptitude tests and I think these are somewhat standard, or increasingly becoming standardised and normal, in big multinational firms' recruitment processes. These aptitude tests can't really be 'revised' or 'prepared' for (though this might be contested). They are basically assessing how your brain works – how it processes information and what sort of skills you have. If you have the 'right' skills according to the aptitude test, then you have a good chance of getting in. If you don't, then sadly, your chances are reduced. However, it is really for jobs where you'll be working with numbers or doing problem-solving skills where performance on these tests really matters. If you don't test well, don't beat yourself up! It's just your cognition which, from what I can tell, is largely a product of biology and genetics and not something you can really control. One way to look at is – if you don't get a job because you are perceived to not have the aptitude for it – it's best to know now and the rejection is a favour. Why work in a career that is not really suited to you, and which will be harder and less fun and less fulfilling than a career that you are suited to? If the aptitude test doesn't work out but the firm like you, might they find another role for you, in a different part of their organisation? A role that is more suited to you? Perhaps.

There are then two further parts of the application process according to my experience, once the interview and aptitude test has taken place. Though these are perhaps specific to types of jobs in types of firms and may not be – probably are not – part of the application process in lots of other employment contexts. First, you spend a day working at the firm. I guess at this point, they're taking a very close look at you. They know they like you, they know you've got the right aptitude. Now they want to see you at work: how well do you listen to instructions? Are you attention to detail orientated? Are you sociable and able to 'fit in'? Perhaps, this phase of the recruitment process is more about attitude rather than aptitude. Second, I went for dinner after work. Again, they're looking closely at you here. Be yourself. Remember interviews and associated things like a trial day at work and dinner after work is not just about 'them' – your prospective employer. It is also about you! You're partly interviewing them: evaluating if this is right for you. You may have other options and offers. But even if you don't, it's a chance to reflect on whether this is what you want. Perhaps, a new role means moving to a new city, leaving friends and family behind. Finding a new place to live. Is it worth doing all that for? This is a two-way process. Like any relationship, you both have to get something out of it. If it's all one way, and exploitative, why bother?

Let's say you fail in your applications. See them as learning opportunities. What can you do next time to increase your chances of getting the sort of job you want? Were you rejected at the application stage? If so, is that a CV issue? Do you need to 'do things' to improve your CV? Are there gaps? Was your application too generic, lacking detail? Did you make clear how you can contribute and emphasise the sorts of skills you have and can bring, and why these skills matter and are relevant now? If not, do so in the future. CVs and covering letters are a chance – the first chance and for some the only chance – to communicate this. Similarly, if you were rejected at the interview stage, can you get feedback? Can you use that feedback to improve your interview technique in the future? Perhaps, you could have been better prepared? If so, prepare better next time! But perhaps the competition was just stronger? Or perhaps it's just a case that while you have loads to offer, you just didn't 'fit' what they wanted for the role this time. If so, then that's fair play.

Now let's say you really, desperately want to work at a particular firm or in a particular sector and that's not happened despite you getting a degree. Is it the end of the road? Not necessarily. You might be desperate to work at Firm X (or think you're desperate to work there). You might go and work at Firm Y for some time, then go back to Firm X in the future, and tell Firm X what experience you have gained at Firm Y and how that can help them. See employment as fluid. It's unlikely you will stay at the same firm for your whole career! This may have once happened, and perhaps if you're recruited to *the* eminent firm in your area after graduating, then you will always stay there, assuming you keep getting promoted and enjoy the work and the working conditions. But the statistics show that graduates of our generation will work for multiple firms, and perhaps in multiple industries. Be strategic, therefore. Play the long game. And see work – whether at an early stage or a later stage in your career – as a step forward to other, better things. Acquire skills and experience as you go. Where you are one day is not where you might end up! Flourish where you're planted, as the saying goes.

Now let's say you get offered a role. The employer comes back with an offer which has a salary stipulated in the contract as well as things like holiday allowance and working expectations, such as the amount of time you're meant to work each week contractually and where you're meant to work from. (There is a feeling that working from home is an expectation and a right these days among some students entering the workplace – they might get a rude awakening). Should you just accept what is put in front of you? You don't want to seem ungrateful or something of a 'diva', with unrealistic expectations. But I'd also be open to negotiating. Can you get a slightly better salary? If working from home is really important to you, can you at least get clarity on their view of it, and something in your contract to enable this? What happens if and when you need paternity or maternity time away from work? What if you get ill – do they have a policy? Try and negotiate the best context you can before you start work – a context that maximises your economic potential and also gives you a framework that is comfortable for you. Know what you're going in to. It should excite you. It should be something that will bring you disappointment if you don't get it!

Others have written in detail about the transition students face as they leave university and enter the world of work. It might be worth reading some of these insights. Perhaps, the best one is Selingo's *There Is Life After College*. This book is written about the American context, but its principles will apply to most national contexts, as well as the American one. Another good read is *The New Rules of Work*. The way the world of work changes – and why that means we have to be fluid and adaptable, especially as we start out in the world of work – really comes through in this book. Another good read is *The Graduate Book* by Chris Davies. It is very career focused, and it's a short read, full of pragmatic insights. *Survive and Thrive* is also worth a read. An advantage of this book is that it talks about life skills – such as budgeting – that those leaving university may not have had time to learn yet, but which they will need to acquire, and acquire quickly, when they leave what may be described as 'the bubble' of university life and enter the exciting but daunting post university environment.

So, back to me. With the job 'in the bag', it's a relief to now be focusing solely on university work and getting the best degree classification that I can, between now and graduating. I enjoy academia. I like the challenge of producing the best work I can and being rewarded for that work in terms of getting good grades and feedback. I am now writing my dissertation. A dissertation is the 'big project' that students write at the end of their degree. We might talk about dissertations in the future, in further email correspondence. I am also preparing for finals: the last exams and assignments that I will do, and which will play such a significant part in the grade I'll get. Year three is the most important as the grades you get in year three – especially semester 2 – are the most significant in determining what grade you'll get. So, I'm doubling down on work. All of the skills I've learned in years two and three are coming to fruition now. The logical thinking, the planning and engaging with lecturers – all that stuff is serving me well. I can see that those students who didn't cultivate key skills earlier in their degrees are really struggling. (These students are also the ones lacking job offers, coincidently or not). Study skills can be compared to the skills of a sportsperson who has spent years cultivating muscle memory. Now that the pressure is on, all those hours of practice are paying off. I'm also doing quite well at controlling anxiety and not having **catastrophic thoughts** ('what if I fail?', 'has this all been a waste of time?', 'will I ever pay off this debt?', etc). I see some around me who aren't managing their emotions well and it is sad to see them struggling so much. I am still mainly getting grades in the 70s and so seem to be heading for a first.

While enjoying the last few weeks of studying and ensuring I do the best I can, conceptually I am ready for the world of work. Some of my friends are going to do master's degrees. Others are going travelling. Some seem to be doing these as they don't know what else to do and have no other options. Some have turned down good jobs (or deferred job offers) to do these things. What suits one individual might not suit others. But for me, I am certain that while I've loved my time here and learned lots and already feel nostalgic for my student days, I am ready for the next chapter of my life. For me that means a career and living in a different, new geographical space.

Anyway, back to work for me.
Be well, Adam.

Eve

Part Two: Work Placements

Adam completes his second year. He passes and proceeds to his third year. Out of the blue, he gets an email from Titus. Adam appreciates that Titus has recontacted him, unprompted. Titus tells Adam more about his experiences working in a placement. The email Titus sent is below.

From: Titus
To: Adam
Subject: Some (more) reflections on my placement year, before we start our third and final year

Just a couple more weeks and we will both be in our third and final year of study, Adam. You'll be proceeding from year two to year three. I'll be going into year three, having had a placement year. Anyway, before I go back to business school to, hopefully, pass my finals and write a strong dissertation in my final year of study, I thought I'd let you know how my year in industry ended up, and what I learned. The last time I emailed you, I was at the start of the placement. I feel I have more to say now about what it's like to work at the sort of firm that graduates like us typically enter. I also want to talk about the sort of people I encountered.

The first observation I made was about the types or groups of people I met at work. It's important to know how these people see work (and by extension people like us – fresh into work) and the impact these people can have on our working lives and attitudes. The first group of people are a small cohort in the firm who I called 'Workaholics'. These are people who seem to prioritise work above all else in their lives. They seem to really like working and like the money and status which their commitment to maybe even obsession with work brings. I can see that these people are very willing to move between firms in order to 'get ahead' and keep progressing their careers. Their commitment to work creates a reputation for them within their industry, so moving between – even being headhunted by – rival firms is quite common for these types. Whether it's healthy to be so committed to work? Whether it's worth perhaps missing out on time with one's family in order to 'deliver' at work? It's not for me to say. But it is a lifestyle choice.

Other people in the organisation may resent workaholics. Workaholics make them look bad and mediocre. The tall poppy syndrome is a thing. You have to admire the stamina of the workaholic and the single-minded focus; their commitment to work despite all it entails on their health, well-being and relationships. But I suppose that if you use work as the main or even only marker of 'success' in life, you're employing a very narrow view of success.

Another group I encountered are made up of employees who work hard, but not as hard as the workaholics. They find a balance between life inside and outside of work. Then there are a small group I call 'slackers'. Perhaps, they were workaholics once, who burnt themselves out, or who didn't get the rewards they feel they deserved, so who have since given up. They are generally well off financially, but they seem bored and angry. Their attitude is nothing to do with me, directly. That's between them and HR. Because they've been in the firm for so long, I guess their positions are secure despite their lack of output. What is my concern though is the impact these people can have on me and others like me, joining the workforce with inexperience and therefore naivety. These people are cynical and resentful so are not ideal colleagues. Don't spend time with them as their attitude might rub off on you. Also, it's not a 'good look' to be seen associating and spending time with people in the firm who are perceived as slackers – people who do as little as possible and who are negative about the firm. Those who are quick to ridicule ideas and resist change but spend their time complaining without ever really suggesting ways forward are there for the pay cheque and to do as little as possible. To be honest, they sap the life out of me. I see them as energy vampires.

As you can probably tell from my other emails, I find it useful and helpful to present 'rules' to make my insights more focused and easier to follow, if you choose to follow them. So, I'll now suggest some rules I think exist in the workplace, which help business students survive a placement year and which will also apply to business school students when they transition from being students to working in 'graduate roles'.

The first rule is networking! I can't believe how important networking is: both within the firm and the industry more broadly. 'It's who you know not what you know' is a saying I used to hear a lot. Having spent time in 'the real world', I know how true this is now. I think I have a decent chance of getting a full-time job at the firm after graduating on the basis that 'I know' key people in the firm and they seem to like me and they know what I am like at work (more on this later – I might have a decision to make). But even everyday things – knowing who to go to in order to get specific tasks done, for example – are all such a vital part of everyday working life. So, network: know who people are, what they do, how you can help them and how they can help you. This is not the same as being a sycophant or seeing people as 'resources' to use for your own means. The latter is abhorrent. We all know those bootlickers in life, even if – sadly – they can get far on the basis of a false charm. I'm talking about letting key people know who you are, what you do and what you can offer. Once you get a good reputation, it's amazing how many opportunities come your way. (It is, partly, because of the importance of networking that I suggest you stay away from the cynical slackers in an organisation

– assuming they exist there – as it signals to people you want in your network that you are or may be a slacker, too, by association).

Be prepared to move (if you can)! By this, I mean move between firms. This applies to business school students who will have the chance to do so having got some work experience after graduating. I learned this rule from speaking to a number of people whom I met during my placement. The way promotions in firms work means that loyalty is not rewarded typically! In other words, by moving to a new firm, you can negotiate to enhance your pay and negotiate a more senior role. Staying in the same firm makes such negotiations less easy. It's counterintuitive. You would think that firms will see loyalty as a good thing and reward those who do well and do well over time. This is the case in some firms. But generally, it is not. Loyalty and competence can be taken for granted. So good, competent and loyal workers will see 'new' people come into the firm, potentially with less credentials and competence but on a higher level! I didn't believe this at first, but I saw it repeatedly during my placement. So, if you want to 'get ahead', don't be afraid to move between firms to accelerate your progression.

That said, if you like the firm and you make 'enough', is a move always best? The grass isn't always greener. Also, moving firms is not as simple as you might think. For example, if you have to move to a new geography, is it worth it? The cost of living in the new place might be higher and could quickly wipe out any apparent financial benefits of moving. What if you have a family? Is it worth moving them – for example, moving children from a school they are settled in and familiar with – to a new one? If you've been at a firm for a number of years, you may have 'rights', such as rights relating to redundancy. You may also have built up funds in a particular pension scheme. By moving between firms, you may lose these rights or have to start in a new, different pension scheme that might be less financially advantageous over the longer term. So, the rule really is don't be afraid to move but move for something that is worth it.

There should be no doubt you're moving to a better, more substantive and exciting role and opportunity. If in doubt, think twice about moving! Also, if you do get a 'better' offer elsewhere, before signing and committing to it, why not speak to your current line manager to see if they will match the new offer? They might not. But if they do, it might help you make a decision about moving, or not moving, that you're more confident about. Their decision to match or not may also signal strongly to you about how they perceive you and your worth!

Another rule: market yourself. I said earlier that you don't want to be sycophantic. You also don't want to come across as conceited, obviously. But if you don't market yourself, it's unlikely anyone else will. In the paragraph above, I talked about how counterintuitive it is that in work, you might have to move between firms to realise your full economic potential. There are reasons for this – one is others are not aware of all you do, or don't appreciate it or are even intimidated because it makes them look less competent comparatively. In turn, you must market yourself. Let people know what you've done – especially if it's been a success. Beware of others trying to take credit for your hard work and ideas! Talk to people to do this. Also, keep a record of your successes and achievements and use them in the future to inform CVs, cover letters and – internal and external – promotion applications. It was the famous American entrepreneur Ted Turner who came up with the quip: 'Early to bed, early to rise, work like hell, and advertise'. This was excellent advice when he said it, and excellent advice now. And the advertising he talks about is just as relevant to self-advertising to those immediately around you as it is to more obvious forms of advertising, linked to marketing products and services to unknown customers!

Another rule that I learned early in the workplace is to do with office politics. The rule on this is simple: avoid them like the plague. Wherever you get people clustered together – and especially when you get people clustered in environments like those in working contexts where there is pressure and competition and, potentially, lots of ego and pride and vanity – you get politics between people. This can take the form of backstabbing and gossiping. It can take the form of exclusion. It can also take the form of brownnosing, like I talked about earlier. Try your best to have nothing to do with any of this! Don't comment on people, even if others are asking you open-ended questions about other colleagues and are seemingly inviting, even demanding, a response from you. It's probably a trap and you're probably being used and manipulated in some larger, weird game of politics and powerplay that you don't even realise is happening, but which could have been going on historically. Go to work – be very professional and focus on your job and what you can control. Be nice to everyone (though don't be a doormat! Stand up to people if you need to and let people know you'll not be exploited and are worth respecting). Don't feel the need to join an 'ingroup'. These groups can disband very quickly. The power that exists among a cohort now may not be in the future. Everyone from the cleaners and receptionists to the CEO should be treated with respect and kindness! This is not just a rule for work, but a rule for life.

Another rule I learned at work is to be agile! Recognise, seize and adapt to opportunities that come your way, with agility and enthusiasm. Don't see any opportunities as 'below you' or 'boring'. As part of this, know where your strengths and weaknesses lie. When an opportunity arises, ensure you explain how you can contribute, but also what you can't do. Try and over-deliver. But don't promise things you can't deliver. You don't want to get a reputation for somebody who promises so much but never delivers, or delivers late or delivers results that are questionable. An older colleague at work told me: 'Find something you're good at and that you enjoy and that there's a need for and that you get paid well for'. I believe that is good advice to follow, at any point in your career. Become specialised at that thing and known for that thing over time. Be the best you can be at that thing!

There is a lot about 'Authenticity' and the 'true self' these days. What this seems to be saying is that you can behave how you want (to an extent) and say what you want (to an extent) and that others should accept you. To a point, I agree with this. But is it really a good idea to be 'your true self' at work all the time? Yes, in some cases. For example, if you have a regional accent, don't change it to 'fit in'. But there is a limit to how much of your true self you should reveal – we are not all as funny and witty and likeable as we might think. Also, the modern workplace is full of ambiguities about what can and cannot be said. I think it's probably a better long-term strategy to be a little less open and a little less expectant of people to embrace – or tolerate – you, no matter what. I think being friendly to colleagues is a good thing – show an interest in them, know what is going on in their lives and remember details. Ask questions about this. But don't talk to every – or even most – colleagues like they're your best friends. You're there to work not to make friends. Keep it polite but professional. Be well mannered. Avoid talking about politics! And even be careful talking about sports. I've seen at work how 'banter' around sports can develop into quite unpleasant conversations and ridicule very quickly, especially when alcohol is consumed on work social evenings. Be nice to others. As you progress, don't dismiss older colleagues who have reached their apex. Don't just befriend those you think will be useful to you.

Another senior colleague – who has been very successful – instructed me not to underestimate the role of luck in your career. Again, this is a good rule. If you get a placement, that is partly luck. The opportunities that come your way? Yes, you make them and have to work at them. But luck played its part. Who you meet, and the extent to which others help and support you? Again, their benevolence is essentially lucky, for you. The series of successes – maybe small successes – that culminate over the years to be meaningful and something one can spin as a 'consistent record of delivering', or some other sort of business jargon are, essentially, a series of lucky coincidences and serendipity. This means that if you're unlucky, don't berate yourself. But also, if you do 'make it', don't get proud, arrogant and conceited. Things may have turned out to be very different, if events had not transpired in ways that were beneficial to you.

When you're starting out at work, especially in a placement year context like the one I'm about to complete, you will be reliant on other people and working closely with other people. This collaboration is necessary for you to learn. If you get the choice of who to work with – and certainly in the future when you may get more say on who you work with – select those you like and can learn from. Work with those you trust and who have integrity. Linked to this, do the jobs you like and which you feel are important.

I mentioned a senior colleague before. Around Christmas, he got me a copy of *The Almanack of Naval Ravikant*. I'm not a fan or advocate of 'how to be happy' books in general. But I did find some wisdom in this book. There are principles linked to wealth and happiness that, as a young person, I feel are worth reading and reflecting on, at this point in our lives, as we start to transition – conceptually if not practically – from university to the world of work, at this formative point in our lives.

Anyway, that's enough from me for now. I will be going on a well-deserved holiday for a couple of weeks, now the placement is over (I will certainly miss the monthly pay cheque) before going back to my third year at business school.

Recently, a couple of colleagues indicated that they see me as a 'good fit' and 'good person' who might have a future at the firm. This has done my confidence the world of good. It has convinced me that all my efforts – from simply getting up every morning and getting the bus to work on time to presenting in front of senior partners at the firm – have been worth it and have been recognised and rewarded not just at a monetary level, but in a deeper, more meaningful way. If it was a job offer or not, I'm not sure. But I think it was certainly a 'if you were to apply to work here full time, we'd look kindly on it and you should demonstrate, in your application, all you've done and learned this year'. I am not sure if I want to work here in the future. But I told them thanks and will certainly look into it.

See you soon, hopefully.
Titus

Summary of Key Points

- Doing paid work while you're a student has advantages – it's a good experience, and you can gain economic capital.
- But doing paid work has 'opportunity costs' – energy and time are finite resources. You don't want to expend too much energy and time on paid work and neglect your studies, especially around assessment submission dates.
- The opportunity to complete a placement year as part of your degree is not suited to everyone! But, for some students, it's a fantastic opportunity to gain experience and pragmatic insight into the world of work and a chance to gain contacts and network. These contacts and networks may prove invaluable when you graduate and are looking for a full-time career.

- Don't rule out forming and running your own business while you're a student! You can 'fit' running the business around your studies. If the business grows substantially, you will have a ready-made enterprise to run when you graduate, with established operations in place.
- Recruitment, especially recruitment into a 'graduate job', typically follows a strict process, from what your CV should look like to what is expected in interviews. Be clear about what the expectations are at each stage.

Things to Think About

- Why might you apply to do a placement year?
- Given how competitive gaining a placement can be, how will you give yourself the best chance of acquiring a placement?
- If you go on a placement, what will your aims be? What, specifically, will you want to learn to do?
- If you're offered a contract with a stipulated salary, will you try and negotiate? Why or why not? If you decide to negotiate, how will you do so?
- How important has 'luck' been in your past and current successes? How important will luck be in your future? Can you construct your own luck?

Exercises/Questions for Discussion

- What types of people does Titus identify as existing in the environment where his placement year unfolds?
- Which groups would you spend time with and look to replicate if you were working there? Who would you look to avoid? Why?
- What impression do you intend to create in your job interview? Why?
- What can you do to ensure you give yourself the best chance of making this impression?

Glossary Terms

Catastrophic thoughts/catastrophic thinking: an affliction that, sadly, seems to be increasingly common among business school students (and business school academics) through which people have a tendency to imagine a very negative outcome, or even the worst-case scenario, and somehow allow this imagined situation to become an imagined 'reality'.

CV: short for curriculum vitae, it is a series of pages that gives prospective employers key information about yourself, such as work experience, qualifications and skills.

Job application: A form and related documents that a business school student will fill in when applying for a job. Don't be tempted to copy and paste information from one application to another. Treat each application as an individual application, with those reading it having their own needs and preferences.

Placement year/sandwich year: a year, normally between years two and three of study, where a student spends a year working in an organisation.

Soft skills: skills – such as managing the emotions of self and others and dressing appropriately – which are not tangible and instantly demonstratable but which are an important aspect of fitting into a working culture.

Further Reading

Cavoulacos, A and Minshew, K. (2020). The New Rules of Work: The Ultimate Career Guide for the Modern Workplace. Orion.

Davies, C. (2018).The Graduate Book: All you need to know to do really well at work. Austin Macauley Publishers.

Jorgenson, E. (2020). The Almanack of Naval Ravikant: A Guide to Wealth and Happiness. Magrathea Publishing

Phillipson, S and Phillipson, J. (2023). SURVIVE & THRIVE: A Graduate's Guide To Life After University. Roots & Wings Ltd.

Selingo, J (2017). There Is Life After College. William Morrow & Company.

5

THE FINAL YEAR OF STUDY

Part One: Study Skills for Year Three

Adam is coming to the end of a lovely summer break, and about to return to university, to complete his third and final year of undergraduate study. He reaches out to Eve, as he aims to prepare himself for the key year approaching. Adam wants to know if there are other dimensions to studying that he should be aware of, which Eve has not yet discussed with him. Eve is now working full-time, but the process of studying – and excelling – in the final year of study is still fresh in her mind and familiar to her. Eve passed her third year with a high first.

From: Adam
To: Eve
Subject: Tips for my final year

Dear Eve,
I'm about to start my third and final year. Your advice and support have served me really well so far. Thank you! So I wanted to ask you about something before I start back at university. (I've had a nice summer, doing a little travelling, a little working and some resting – which I think I really needed). I managed to get an average of 61 at the end of year 2. So, I am right on the cusp of getting a 2:1, but will need to do (at least) that well again in year three to secure a 2:1, which is the grade I – and seemingly everyone else – really want. Perhaps, getting advice from you and applying it will secure the 2:1 I want.

DOI: 10.4324/9781003467397-6

My question is: are there any other dimensions of academic life I should know about but that you've not told me about in your earlier emails? Might there be any specific aspects of university life that I should be aware of? This is not to say that I've perfected – or I'm even comfortable with – some of the other skills you've mentioned in earlier emails, like critical thinking. These are ongoing skills I'll have to work on for the rest of my life if I'm going to acquire and master them. 'Lifelong learning' is the phrase I've heard to refer to ongoing skill development. But it is to say that if there are other things to think about at this point, I'd like to at least be aware of them. The third year is so crucial. An average of two or three per cent over the year can be the difference between a grade boundary for me. I need to try and get the odds in my favour!

Thanks so much,
Adam

From: Eve
To: Adam
Subject: RE: Tips for my final year

Hello there – lucky you, taking a well-deserved rest over the summer! The brain is like a muscle. It needs work to get stronger and better. But it also needs rest to recover and actually grow and come to function, and for all the hard work to be visible and pay off. By resting your brain now, you will go into the third year fresh and rested.

I'd break the year into two. See part one as the period between September to Christmas (semester 1). This needs to be a period of focused, sensible and hard work, with work being orientated around getting the best grades you can. Then you get another rest. Then there is the final hard slog – the last period, between Christmas and handing in your **dissertation** in the early summer. Get your head around this structure and rhythm. Break the chronology down into two manageable time frames or 'chunks', with a definite 'end point' and a definite 'rest period' in the middle.

Of course, structuring the year like this, into two clear parts with rest periods built in, is something of an idealistic plan. It assumes you don't become unwell, or that people around you don't become unwell or that a tragedy doesn't strike. We can't always assume that normality continues. If catastrophic things happen, you have options and you should look into them! Such as telling the university and asking them to consider giving you extensions on your work or even taking into account these circumstances when assessing your work. The business school is there to support you, and I know from experience that they are very sympathetic to cases where students have had genuine, unexpected challenges arise.

The first thing I want to say about 'new' skills to acquire and apply in the final year is actually more about the way you 'break down' academic material and information to get the most bang for your buck. This means thinking about the question: of all the information available to me that I've read, which bits of information are the most salient and useful in terms of applying to what I'm doing now? Be very disciplined and strict. I'm talking here mainly in relation to writing assignments and using what you read in journal articles and books to answer these assessments. I'm also assuming that you're reading relevant material; so, reading that is prescribed to you via reading lists from module leaders. You can't use all you read to help inform your assignment, obviously. Instead, the information you read can be **taxonomised** into three types. First, there is information that is irrelevant to you in terms of this assessment. This does not mean the information is intrinsically irrelevant. It may interest you. It may be highly applicable to another assignment. But for the purposes of the assignment, you're doing now, it's not important. So discard it. Reject it. Be brutal. Don't let something that seems 'linked' to what you're writing distract you. Only engage with the information you read if it really helps you frame what you're writing or evidence what you're saying. Does this bit of information actually relate to what I'm saying – something very specific in the assignment – to back up the point I'm making? Or is it just related in a rather tenuous way. If it's the latter, get rid of it. The best assignments are laser-like in their focus. They don't go off on tangents. Each paragraph has a purpose, and each sentence in that paragraph should play a part.

Then there is information that is relevant and worth including, but which isn't so relevant and important as to make a huge deal of it. I'm thinking here about key references or even references with page numbers that you use to evidence and substantiate a key point you're making. This information will get you grades and should be taken seriously and can be seen as foundational information that you engage with. So, for example, let's say you want to make a point that a number of scholars have looked at an area. Choose key references that are examples of scholars doing this. Then put their names and the dates of the studies in brackets via a simple citation. This gives context. It shows those grading your work that you're aware of these key citations and have engaged with them. Generally, information of this sort will typically come in the introduction of your work; as it gives a level of context and framing, it justifies your contribution and roots your contribution to the wider literature.

Third, there is the sort of information that you'll come across which is integral and fundamental to you, and which can help your work in a really fundamental way. This is not just work as above; it gives important context. This is work within that work; a sentence or paragraph that is a statement that is worth affirming and emphasising; because doing so helps locate your work and focus its analysis. Typically, this will be a direct quotation that sums up your position or justifies your work in a seminal way, and which lays the foundations for the rest of the work to emerge. It's a justification for the work, from which you can package all arguments and contributions.

For example, you might find a recent quote given by a leading scholar in the field, in a leading journal, calling for work that does a certain thing or shedding light on a topic in a specific way. Assuming you go on to respond to this – that is using the call to justify what you're doing – it makes sense to use this quote verbatim to frame your contribution. You may even return to this quote in your conclusion to remind readers of not just what you did but why you did it. For example, in the intro you may say something like:

'author C (year and page number) notes that "more work is needed which looks at this phenomenon in the context of developing economies, given the onus to date on investigating it in developed economies." Further, Author D suggests work in this area adopts a qualitative focus, to complement existing work that uses a quantitative approach. As put by Author D (year and page number): "to give further context to this area, work that takes a qualitative approach is required so that richer contextual understandings of how this phenomenon is lived are needed"'.

Building on a statement like this, you can then say something like 'in response, this work looks at the emerging economy of Z and adopts a qualitative approach to answer the question N'. Then, in the conclusion, you may say something like: 'aware of calls in existing literature for qualitative work (Author D) to emerge which focuses on different sorts of economies and contexts than those studied to date (author C), this essay has', then state what you did. Engaging with academic materials in this way allows clear, cohesive and focused analysis to emerge which builds on and is rooted in established, conventional literature and ideas. By engaging with academic material in these ways and breaking that material down in ways that serve you and allow your analysis to unfold, you give your work a better chance of entering the high 60s and 70s. You're also signalling to those grading the work right from the start that this student understands what is being asked and makes clear how they will respond to it. First impressions last. If you go on to do what you claim, you've engaged with academic material in a way that will get you into the 70s in your third year.

As I said, the above suggestions about engaging with academic material are rooted mainly in the assumption that you're reading journal articles and books, and – even more than that – reading journal articles that are relevant because your module leaders have suggested you read them. They are thus suitable for the level of study you're at (third-year material is more complex than first-year material

– that simple SWOT analysis you did in year one might not have enough rigour in year three!). Other than journal articles and books, the only other source of information that I saw students do well through engaging with in the third year are official statistics. For example, students might use official statistics to tell a story around business start-ups, how rates of startups differ at the level of gender or how many businesses fail in this geography compared to that geography according to statistics. These statistics are credible and can inform analysis. In contrast, I strongly advise against using media sources (and even very basic things like dictionary definitions). I was stunned to see students, even in their third year and having been warned not to do this in years two and three, continue to use things like online newspaper reports to underpin their 'analysis'. Using such sources gives the impression that your preparation is underdeveloped and weak and makes your analysis overly general and lacking in depth. I suppose the temptation to do this is that by using an online media source, you simplify debates and ideas and appear to shortcut work, by providing 'evidence' that is schematic and saving you the time and energy of reading more demanding literature, such as that in journals.

Ultimately, the importance of engaging with the right sort of information in the right way is linked to constructing credible academic arguments and analyses. How well you do in year three – so whether the prospect of getting that 2:1 you so desire materialises or not – is linked to how viable the academic arguments and analysis you put forward are. Use what you read to provide a coherent, substantive analysis that is rooted in the question. Think about what you're being asked and respond to that. I was surprised in year three when I spoke to some course-mates who didn't do well in assignments. When they got feedback, they were told they'd not addressed the question that was set. They'd even set their own questions in some cases, deviating from what they were asked to do and instead doing what they wanted. Avoid this mistake and use what you read to systematically bolster your analysis.

Of course, to get into the position where you've read enough relevant material to distinguish between whether what you've read is irrelevant, relevant generally or relevant intrinsically to your assignment(s) and the ongoing need to construct creditable academic arguments, you will have to do a high volume of reading. Some people like to read, some don't. Some find reading a pleasure but others find reading very time-consuming and energy zapping. When reading for a business school assignment, it's not like reading leisurely, as you might on holiday around a pool, immersed in some entertaining novel which takes little concentration to follow. Instead, reading academic material to construct creditable arguments and locate relevant information means reading in a focused way: seeing what is written down, following the logic and trends of what is presented but also always thinking does this – what I'm reading – matter to me now, and if so how and why? What is the utility of this reading? Further, what you're reading is probably written in a dense, complex – even pompous – way. To help 'cope' with both the volume of reading and the nature of what you're reading – at university generally and in your third year in particular – I suggest doing two things. First, take breaks. Read an article, or even sections of the article, then have a rest. Second, highlight and note which bits of information that you're reading are especially useful to you. Don't expect to memorise everything you read. Instead, highlight what is relevant. Either read articles and books electronically, in PDF formats, and highlight what you want on the article, or print the articles out, and read while highlighting with a pen. That way, you can revisit the article, see what you've highlighted and decide if what you've highlighted is relevant and, if so, what to do with it now. You might even highlight in different colours, to help categorise what you've highlighted; for example, highlighting methodological points you find relevant in one colour and theoretical points in another.

All this reading is hard work. Evolving what you read into information that underpins an assignment is even harder. No wonder, then, that some students fall into the deadly trap of **plagiarism**. This is where you submit work that is not your own but which you pretend to be. There's a range here, from using bits of other people's work all the way to submitting entire assignments that other people have written. It's highly dishonest. It's also a very flawed approach. One lecturer told me that when they grade work, they see certain bits of information alongside the work. One key bit of information is generated for them through computer software, and it reveals how much of the essay resembles any other submission, at any other university, in history. Therefore, essays that have plagiarism at their core are identified early. Students can be expelled for plagiarism. The risk is just not worth it. Simply don't do it!

Another area that I think you should be aware of is AI. AI is fast-paced, emerging and changing all of the time. Its consequences on studying at a business school are fluid, then. But what some students seem to be doing now is asking AI to produce entire assignments for them, which they submit. Again, this might seem like a cunning way around the system, and a chance to bypass all the taxing reading and work that producing an assignment requires. It's not, though! Like most things that seem to offer so much for so little investment, the prospect of AI constructing an essay for you, that will receive a top grade, is too good to be true. As well as being dishonest, the AI software can't (yet) synthesise information in the form of suggested reading. What is offered, then, is an essay that appears well written and which sounds impressive, but which has an overgeneralised answer which is void of the literature that the module leader has asked you to engage with. Therefore, the essay will almost certainly get a poor grade (at best) as it's too far away from what was set, asked and expected.

The penalties for submitting work that is not yours vary. Whether what you submit is generated via AI or whether it's written by someone else is irrelevant.

What is relevant is that you've 'cheated'. You've submitted work while trying to deceive others that it's yours. The penalty for doing so may be different at different universities. Generally though, you will be expelled, or given a formal warning that if you do it again, you will be expelled.

In short – don't do it!

Eve

Part Two: The Dissertation

Adam is very happy with the advice he receives. He is confident that he can utilise what Eve has said. He is starting to feel a little anxious about the prospect of writing a dissertation. He remembers talking to course-mates about dissertations in year two. It carries a lot of importance in terms of grades. He asks Eve for more advice, specifically about the dissertation process.

From: Adam
To: Eve
Subject: RE: Tips for my final year

Thanks Eve, that's all interesting and helpful. Can I also ask you about the dissertation? I know it's a long way off (or it feels like a long way off now, as I won't start writing the dissertation until semester 2 of year 3). But the dissertation carries a mystique, aura and challenge around it, so I want to start conceptualising it. I wonder if you're able to give me some pointers to think about how I should approach the dissertation. What was your experience of doing a dissertation like?

Adam

From: Eve
To: Adam
Subject: RE: Tips for my final year

Ah, yes, the **dissertation**. It's good that you're already thinking about it, though you should try not to let it cause you anxiety. As you've identified, it is a very important part of your degree and a determinant (though not the only determinant) of what grade you will leave with. So, let me try and describe the dissertation process – and it is a process that unfolds over time – in as much depth as possible. Before doing so, I want to say: enjoy the process. I felt daunted and intimidated at the start of the dissertation process – so did most of my course-mates, I'm sure. But we almost all agreed that once the dissertation was written and submitted, the process was quite enjoyable and the anxiety we had felt at the start proved undue and excessive.

So, the dissertation. The first thing to say is that your relationship with your **dissertation supervisor** is really important. Try and cultivate a good relationship with them. More important, perhaps, is the topic you choose. Think about two things. First, have you learned anything or come across any-thing in years one and two that really interest you? If so, I wonder if you can focus your dissertation on this area/these areas. There was a particular topic I liked (business growth) and I also enjoyed studying gender. In the end, I did a dissertation on how gender relates to business growth. This was a good choice. I always preferred qualitative work, so I used a qualitative framework to underpin my research. Also, if you get a chance to choose your supervisor, was there a particular lecturer who you found engaging and who you'd like to supervise you? Cynically, is there a supervisor who is known to be a 'soft' marker? Maybe it's worth trying to work with them, from a grades point of view.

We had to propose a dissertation title and topic. I guess you will too. This happens before you start the dissertation properly. The proposal doesn't have to be particularly refined at the start. I suggest thinking about what interests you generally and what concepts or theories you've learned about and trying to weave a title and proposal together based on that. As things move forward, you can refine the title and topic and your supervisor should help you do this.

Another key issue is the methodology: will you be doing a qualitative or qualitative piece of work? I guess it's really important to choose the approach that suits your learning style and skills the best. Also, make sure you get ethical approval to do the research before you start!

One thing I found helpful when I talked to my supervisor was to do <u>with research gaps</u> – the dissertation should find a gap, if possible, and try and fill it. So, there should be a justification for why you're doing this work – why is it important? What gap(s) do you fill by doing this research? (Think about what I said earlier about 'framing' and justifying your essay, and apply it here to your dissertation). The best work, I was told, has a really narrow question and focus, with a strong justification for this focus. From here, the work evolves in relation to this narrow question. Also, your dissertation should 'add' or contribute to existing literature – so saying something new or testing/adding to/disproving some accepted wisdom in the field.

Having located a question that is worth pursuing – and that literature shows is worth pursuing – and which your supervisor agrees as worth pursuing and having figured out which methodological approach is the best one for you and the best one to answer your question, then your dissertation will unfold over a structure. I will talk about the structure my dissertation took, as this is a typical one. Note, I start by discussing chapter 2, for reasons I will come to.

Chapter 2 of my dissertation was a **literature review** – literally, I reviewed some key articles (and books) in my area. I was told not to review everything! Just a few key articles, explaining what they said. It was amazing to see how ideas came together for me once I read around the topic. What has been said about this area? How will your project relate to what has been said? Will your project go in a new direction? Will it elaborate on a very specific, nuanced question already asked? Will it ask a new question? Leave the reader feeling that you know what others have said about the area and you know how your project will add utility to the area.

I was then able, in chapter 3, to explain my methods: how I got data, which in my case was through interviews and also how I systematically analysed data. Perhaps, you can add to the field through some sort of innovative methodology, generating data that is different from that which previous studies have used. Perhaps, you're replicating the methodological approach others have taken. At the undergraduate level, you don't need some complex methodological innovation to occur in your work! You just need to explain why the approach you've selected makes sense and that you've collected and analysed data in a way that complies with established, accepted academic norms.

Chapter 4 was a findings chapter, so I explained what I found out through my interviews: what did the transcripts I collected reveal, which was important to my research question, and how did the way I analysed data allow me to present findings that are valid? Your findings will be unique to your project and the particular methodology you applied. (Later on in the dissertation's conclusion, you can explore how future findings might emerge and be useful.)

Chapter 5 was a discussion, explaining/analysing why what I found out mattered in relation to *the literature I reviewed*. This required me to revisit chapter 2 and engage again with the literature I reviewed and make clear claims on how my data related to it.

From here, my supervisor told me to 'top and tail' the work, through a conclusion (chapter 6), which does not just summarise the work but considers future research questions, limitations of this project and practical implications of the work. There is also an introductory chapter (chapter 1) which I was told to write last (you'll be able to introduce the work better in chapter 1 once you know what the contribution is). The introduction should frame the work, explain why it's important, define a research question (remember, the tighter and more specific the question, the better in general) and introduce readers to the structure of the dissertation.

In short, this is the structure my supervisor suggested I follow, and it might help you:

TABLE 5.1 Dissertation Structure

Chapter	Aim	Tips
1. Introduction	To introduce the work. Explaining the aims of the work, identifying a research question and explaining why the question matters. Navigate readers.	Write at the end.
2. Literature Review	Review/discuss a number of key texts (literature) linked to your area, before explaining how you will develop them/build on them. This is a key chapter.	Do this first! You will be amazed how much easier the work is once you know the literature. Try and review up-to-date research and if you find a published 'review' article of the field, this will be very helpful in contextualising the field. Try and identify an area in literature where others call for more work, and use that call to frame your contribution.
3. Methodology	Explain here how you got data, how you analysed data and also the 'fit' between what my dissertation supervisor called *epistemology and methodology*; in other words, the fit between what you aim to do in terms of generating knowledge and how you got data to fulfil that aim.	Choose the research approach (qualitative or quantitative) that suits your learning style/ strengths as well as the epistemological aims of your dissertation. You will probably get lectures on research methodology – attend these, paying attention to notions like research philosophy/ ontology.

(*Continued*)

TABLE 5.1 (Continued)

Chapter	Aim	Tips
4. Findings	Present what you found out. If you can show that what you found out has been arrived at systematically in terms of data analysis, that is a good thing. Also, note the difference between generating knowledge (based on your data) *inductively* and *deductively*.	Using software packages (e.g. SPSS for statistics or NVivo for qualitative data coding) can be a good way of making the findings you present appear more rigorous.
5. Discussions/Analysis	Discussions should be focused on analysing – this is *showing – why what you found out in the previous chapter matters.* This is not just a repetition of your findings, but a detailed discussion of how your	In some dissertations, it might be helpful to use a table to explain how your data contributes to extant literature.
6. Conclusion	findings (your data) relate to the literature you reviewed in chapter 2, and how the data shows that you've fulfilled your research aims. This is the final chapter, where you reflect on the work, placing it in a larger context.	Chapter 6 does not summarise what has already come but concludes by identifying future research areas, practical implications and also limitations.

I also want to say that, after the process, it became clear that the markers wanted to make sure I showed *the skills they wanted me to show*. They expected me to write clearly, review literature and demonstrate that I can gather and analyse data and say something about the data in relation to the field. BUT they did not expect some sort of pioneering, groundbreaking piece of research. It's just a UG dissertation and they see lots of them. So, in some way, take the pressure off yourself. My dissertation was 12,000 words. I was told to write around 1,000 words in the intro and 750 words or so for a conclusion: with the rest of the work constituting those key middle chapters. You can use an appendix for things like interview transcripts and visuals. Also, make sure your work passes **ethical tests** before commencing.

You will also need to write an **abstract** (one-page summary of the work, again do this at the end), a **bibliography** where all the work you reference is cited (see my other email on this which I sent to you in your first year when you were struggling with essays) and an acknowledgements page, where you thank people – it's probably a good idea to thank our supervisor here as well as friends and family.

Before signing off, I should add that the dissertation process has been written about extensively. In addition to what I've said, it might be a good idea to read around the topic more widely. To do this, I suggest reading Cottrell's (2014) work called *Dissertations and Project Reports: A Step by Step Guide*. Another work that students in my cohort found helpful is Greetham's (2019) *How to Write Your Undergraduate Dissertation*. Greetham also wrote a book called *How to Write Your Literature Review*. As I said above, the literature review is a very important but difficult part of the dissertation. This book – focusing entirely on the literature review – can be a Godsend for some students, grappling with the complexities of reviewing literature). A less well-known book, but one course-mates found useful, is Swetnam and Swetnam's (2000) *Writing Your Dissertation*. By engaging with these works, and through interacting with your supervisor, I am confident that you will find answers to any questions that emerge during the dissertation process.

Anyway, I hope I've answered your questions. Good luck with the process of writing the dissertation and completing your degree. Be confident and enjoy your final year!

Eve

Summary of Key Points

- You can conceptualise the academic year as having two main parts – with Christmas in between. This makes the academic year more manageable, in terms of workload and your own psychological well-being. Don't feel like you can't rest between the two parts of the academic year! In fact, it is beneficial to do so. Don't feel like you're sinking! There are discernible points or milestones in the year, and you just need to focus on these, one at a time.
- Not all the information you read and use in your assignments is of equal importance! Engage more with work that will get you higher grades (i.e. work clearly related to the assessment) instead of work that is of less importance. A key skill to learn at university, which you will almost certainly use in your life after business school, is the skill of being able to select and identify pertinent information and use it in particular ways, while rejecting information that does not further your aim, at this point.

- When choosing a dissertation topic, ensure you choose a topic that interests you, and which your supervisor approves. Try and identify a clear research gap and allow this gap to underpin your dissertation in terms of explaining why the dissertation matters and how the dissertation contributes to existing knowledge and literature. It is often a good idea to revisit any topic you studied earlier – for example, a topic you learned about in a lecture or even a topic you studied for assessment purposes – and then use that topic as the primary focus of your dissertation. There will be an established body of scholarship already on this area; so, why not revisit it and use it to inform your dissertation?

Exercises/Questions for Discussion

- Is achieving a first or a 2:1 really that important to you? Why/why not?
- Are there any things you might do in year three, especially in terms of producing assessed work, in order to bolster the grade you get?
- How will you establish and determine which information – of all the vast amount of information that is available to you – is the most relevant to you, when preparing a particular assignment?
- In terms of the dissertation process, why is your relationship with your dissertation supervisor so important? How will you cultivate a healthy, positive working relationship with your dissertation supervisor? In particular, how will you establish expectations? For example, expectations around when drafts of chapters will be sent from you to your supervisor and how long it will take for your supervisor to review the work you sent and give feedback?

Glossary Terms

Abstract: a short – normally no more than one page – statement presented at the start of your dissertation. The abstract should summarise the main points of the dissertation, such as what it's about, why it's needed, how you collected and analysed data (methodology), the main findings your methodology revealed and how what you found out contributes to existing theory and literature. If any practical or policy recommendations emerge in your dissertation, these can be included in the abstract, too. It is always a good idea to write the abstract after you've written the rest of the dissertation. This will allow you to provide a fuller abstract, when the work is fresh in your mind and when you can be clear and specific about what the dissertation represents. It should incentivise readers to read the work and make clear to those examining the work what will emerge, and why.

Bibliography: the list at the end of an assessment, which gives readers details of all the references that you have used, or cited, in the assessment.

Dissertation   A project that you write in the second semester of your final year of study.

Dissertation supervisor: the member of the academic staff allocated by the business school to supervise your dissertation. They will normally arrange a series of meetings with you, in which they will discuss aspects of your dissertation. Your supervisor usually grades the dissertation you write, alongside a 'second marker'. The average grade, proposed by the supervisor and the second marker, is usually the grade awarded to the dissertation. The supervisor should, ideally, be a member of staff with some knowledge of the topic you're writing about and the methodological approach that underpins your dissertation.

Ethical tests: it is vital that all research adheres to ethical standards, practices and 'tests'. The same is true of any research you participate in as part of your dissertation process. It is crucial that no harm will come to any people who participate in your research, for example, any people whom you interview. Hence, you must not ask questions that are offensive or overly personal/familiar in interviews. Likewise, you must not preproduce quotes in your work that could land the respondent in trouble. It might be best to anonymise the people you research by using pseudonyms to refer to them and their businesses. Those who participate in your research should consent to take part in it, normally by signing a consent form, which details to them what your work is about and how any data they pass on to you will be used. You must not conduct research with children or other vulnerable people, unless special ethical clearance has been granted. No harm should come to those you research. You should not put yourself in danger when conducting research, for example interviewing members of the public you don't know or going to places to do research where you're not safe.

Literature review: to paraphrase an advert that was fashionable not too long ago – this is exactly what it says on the tin; namely a review of literature. In this context, literature refers to the articles and books that make up the 'literature' on a topic; a collective body of knowledge, produced by subject experts. A chapter in your dissertation should review the literature on the area you're writing about. A literature review normally occurs in chapter 2. Readers should have a thorough understanding of what literature says on a topic, having read your review. This might include debates on a topic and key questions that others have identified. Some areas have vast literatures attached to them. Do not try and review all the literature. Rather, review a smaller number of key sources. Key tip: some authors produce what are called 'review articles', where an author provides a thorough review of a field. This review will normally be published in a peer-reviewed journal. If you find a review article linked to the area your dissertation looks at (or choose a topic in response to a review article) much of the 'hard work' has already been done: a literature review already exists. You can use a review article to help structure your literature review, by making clear how your data adds to or contributes to or 'brings on' or even challenges existing literature and knowledge within it. Key tip two: to organise your literature review, it is often helpful to use subheadings. So, if your dissertation is looking at sports, marketing or online marketing, it is useful to review three bodies of literature and then make clear how and why your dissertation is bringing all of these areas together.

Plagiarism: the process of submitting work that is not yours but which you claim to be yours to deceive those marking, with the view of receiving grades for that work. In worst cases, the plagiarised work will be an assessment the student has bought, which has been written by a ghostwriter. Also, AI may have been used to construct an answer that is plagiarized. Penalties for students who submit plagiarised work are, rightly, harsh and business schools are becoming more and more sophisticated at recognising submitted plagiarised work submitted by students.

Taxonomize (information):   this is where information is grouped into more specific categories. For example, if one reads a lot on management, they might see themes like 'the role of gender in management', 'the role of class in management' and 'learning from past failures' existing in what they read. Taxonomizing information (e.g. placing information into smaller themes) allows a larger body of thought to be grouped into simpler, potentially more manageable, sections, which can have practical and conceptual benefits in terms of doing things with the information (such as using it for assignments).

Further Reading

Cottrell, S. (2014). Dissertations and Project Reports: A Step by Step Guide. London: Macmillan Study Skills.

Greetham, B. (2019). How to Write Your Undergraduate Dissertation. London: Bloomsbury Study Skills.

Greetham, B. (2020). How to Write Your Literature Review. London: Macmillan Study Skills.

Swetnam, D and Swetnam, R. (2000). Writing Your Dissertation: The bestselling guide to planning, preparing and presenting first-class work. How to Books.

6

THE GRADUATE

Part One: Reflecting on the Degree

Having finally graduated, Adam writes to both his friends to thank them for their support and advice over the course of his degree.

From: Adam
To: Eve; Titus
Subject: Thanks for everything!

Dear Eve and Titus,
I am emailing you both (have you two ever even met?) because you both provided such informative advice during my time as a student, and I want to thank
you and let you know how I did, and what I'm thinking now.

I did it – I completed my degree. I am now a university graduate. I got a 2:1
in the end. I got a particularly high grade for my dissertation (high for me anyway, in the high 60s). This pushed my average up, to a 64 overall, which is
solidly in the upper second category. I am delighted. I really needed this to
work out. I know a degree is not some sort of golden ticket: there will still be
problems in the world, and I have to now undergo that transition from student
to the next version of me. Life must go on and having a degree does not make
me special or unique. But I am so proud of myself. I have gained so much confidence. I think that in my working life in the future, when I get challenges, I will
think back to now and tell myself you did it then – overcoming challenges and

DOI: 10.4324/9781003467397-7

getting results – and you can do it again. It's been a journey for me. It's been a journey for all my course-mates.

I handed in my dissertation, as the last act at university. At that point, I'd completed all the assessments for all my other modules. I waited to hear how I did for around 3 weeks. Then, I got an email from the **board of examiners**, which – as you might know – is a board of people, mainly academics, who look at every student and how they did in every module and come to a decision on what each student's final degree classification should be. (The board also meet to discuss year one and two students, deciding on or confirming whether they can proceed to the next stage of study or not). I'll exit the business school with an upper second (a 2:1). This gives me options. I can apply for certain jobs, such as graduate schemes that require a 2:1. I can do further study. I'll talk about these options more below. Some course-mates are dismayed that they didn't get a 2:1 (i.e. an average in the 60s). But there is hope for them. In time, they will see this. It's not a simple binary distinction, meaning a student with a 2:1 or a first is somehow worthy and deserving of a golden future, while those with a 2:2 or lower should despair.

I want to make a point about students on my course who I know and who ended up with borderline average grades, like 58s and 69s. So, we know that an average in the 60s is a 2:1, an average in the 70s is a first, etc.

What impressed me was that for *some* students on the borderline between degree classifications, the board of examiners exercised **discretion**. Instead of taking a black-and-white view that saw them 'cut off' grades, they awarded some borderline cases a higher degree category despite not being in that category intrinsically. For example, a friend who averaged 58 got a 2:1 (despite not being in the 60s), and a friend with 69 got a first (despite not being in the 70s). I think this is a more pragmatic and understanding way to award certain students certain degrees than a cutoff point that might be too arbitrary and simplistic. The board have discretion. They will 'bump up' a student, sometimes, because of that student's '**exit trajectory**', which means that the student's work has improved over time. This improvement came late but suggests that the student is working at a level now, despite not working there earlier. So, that improvement is taken into account when awarding a grade (e.g. four modules at the end of semester 2 may be in the 70s, despite much earlier work in the low 60s. This means the grade is in the 60s but this is a '70s level' student at the time of exit). Other times, the board bumped up students into a higher-grade category because one or two modules severely held the students' average back. For example, a student who consistently gets low 60s but who gets a couple of grades in the 40s has their average pulled down (to the higher 50s). But they will not necessarily be penalised too harshly for the anomalous grades in those two modules that 'pull them down'. Instead, the board looks at the wider spread of grades in order to gauge and ascertain a truer, more objective category for the individual student in question. While, technically, the students are in one grade category, a closer inspection reveals the student may be in another, higher category. I liked this notion of discretion. It seems fair.

Though discretion is not a rule for everyone – each case is treated individually. Someone in the mid-50s or 60s will not get bumped up! It is for those borderline cases. When the board of examiners meet to discuss progression and degree classifications, **external examiners** are present. These examiners are academics who are based at another business school, who have wider experience in higher education and who are appointed to objectively ensure the business school in question acts in line with wider rules and regulations. This adds further assurance that the process of award allocation is rigorous. So, if discretion is used in one case, and not in another, the examiners may flag this up and ask why and ensure consistency. Overall, students can have faith in the process.

Stepping back from the final outcome, and the rather nerdy – but to me fascinating – process that sees how and why students are awarded the classification of degrees they get, I've been reflecting on the entire course over the years and my time as a student and what I've learned about the whole process. The first thing is how quickly time seems to have gone by. I know that objectively it's been 24 hours a day and 60 minutes an hour! But experientially it's flown by. I guess the phrase is time flies when you have fun. People did say things like 'enjoy it, it'll be over before you know it'. I now know what they meant.

I am also amazed at the extent to which I declined and self-sabotaged in my first year. It really was touch and go for me. I was immature. I was almost kicked out. But I learned from it. And in the end, I did ok. In a way, the aspect of the degree that I am most proud of is the way I bounced back from the situation I was in during semester 2 of year 1. I became so much more organised and mature in years two and three. It sounds corny, but it represents my own comeback story.

It took me a while to settle into university life. But now, having been here for so long, I feel very at home – even institutionalised. I know we all settle and integrate at different speeds. But I really think that those who settle into university life quickly are at an advantage – those who miss home too much and dwell on the past and are reluctant to embrace the new opportunity in front of them are, to me, analogous to a boxer trying to fight with one hand tied behind their back. It was strange to see people who were 'big fish' at school struggle so much at university, where they suddenly went from higher performers at school to ordinary students. Despite my initial pensive start, there is a large part of me that does not want to move on. I fear I may live in the past instead of embracing 'now' and the future. I know some students can't wait to leave and start working. Eve, I remember you telling me that you felt that way when your degree ended. But I'm not there.

That said, I am not like some people I know, who are crying and heartbroken because this part of their life is over. University is a formative time. And the period immediately after it is formative too. In terms of employment on the basis of the degree, I guess there is a small window to really optimise the qualifications I have. Let's be honest, in a year from now there will be thousands of other recent graduates, like me now. If I am getting a job, it's best to do it earlier, before the job market becomes even more saturated, as it will be a year from now, with another cohort of new graduates entering it.

Another thing that I've realised – after all this time – is that the business school was always on my side. (I guess the proclivity for a business school to help its students and do its best for them, in ways that may be hidden, is evidenced in the ways 'discretion' is applied, as discussed above). My lecturers were for me, not against me. Perhaps, I was paranoid, but I often – even always – had the false sense that they were, in assignments, trying to 'catch me out' or 'trick me'. I sometimes worried I was an inconvenience to them. Some seemed unapproachable, especially the more intimidating ones. But I now realise I was wrong about this. They always wanted me to do well. They are in their jobs because, for the most part, they want to pass on knowledge, are passionate about the subject and want to educate and inform future generations. They are overworked and have to manage hundreds of students. But they are fair, impartial and objective and when I look back to my interactions, I can see what they told me was academically correct and told in good faith. (By the way, those lecturers who seemed the most intimidating were often the most approachable and helpful – it is those who terrified me in the first few lectures whom I approached for job **references**, and those are the ones who have taken the time to write good, specific and clear references for me, which I'm using to try and get a job – more on jobs below).

The other thing I realised, perhaps too late, is how many opportunities I had just by virtue of being enrolled at a university and having access to the university campus and its facilities. I had opportunities not just to learn 'on' my course, but to learn more broadly. For example, to learn languages. I also had opportunities to get involved in university societies and clubs. I wish I had now. I only found out the other week that there is a pool and gym on campus! I would have enjoyed that. Perhaps, I had the attitude that I'm 'too cool for school' and that these things were somehow below me. I was wrong. I think I would have learned loads and met a more diverse set of friends if I'd embraced my identity as a student. Perhaps, I found it hard to shake the identity of the person I was before I came here. On reflection that was a mistake.

The reality is that I have debt – it was expensive to study. Some may say a luxury to study. But this debt is interesting. I only have to pay it back when I make a certain amount. (As things stand, if I never make a certain amount, I never have to pay the debt! Though this seems harsh on taxpayers, who have essentially paid for me to study). Even if I do start paying this debt because I 'make enough', the debt repayments will come off my wages in relation to what I earn. Repayments won't be crippling. Slowly and surely, the debt will be reduced while I hate the debt, the nature of the debt is quite unique, and I like to see it as an investment. It's not like debt on a depreciating asset, like that on a new car. That said, I want the debt paid off, as soon as possible.

I also learned what a strange relationship I had with work. I don't think this is exclusive to me. The pattern went like this. I didn't always engage with my work. When I did, especially in year one, I did so out of necessity – because deadlines were approaching. I didn't really want to engage with work. I assumed it would be 'boring' or 'hard'. I saw those who were enthusiastic as 'nerdy' and 'geeky'. What an immature and myopic view! When I started engaging with work, out of necessity and in a state of panic, I felt confused. However, when I started engaging with work at a deeper level – taking my time and not rushing, thinking systematically about what I need to do and how to best do it – I realised that I really enjoyed a lot of the work I did. I don't claim to love it. But it was interesting work. It's true that you get out what you put in. I think that if I'd had a more genuine desire and hunger to learn and work right from the start, I would have achieved more in terms of grades and enjoyed the course more as an intellectual pursuit. It is for this reason that I'd encourage people to study what genuinely interests them. Don't study what others say you should.

I guess in the modern world, we are always surrounded by distractions to fill our time and take our thoughts, energy and attention away from us, especially away from our work and other positive things we are meant to be doing – the sorts of things Titus suggested around optimising our bodies and minds, those vessels that are so integral to our well-being and which are so integral to how we perform as business school students. These distractions tend to be rooted in technological mediums. It's a lot more appealing and easy – in terms of energy expenditure and concentration – to turn on a television or open up your phone than it is to read a journal article and think about that article's utility within an assignment! (Coincidentally, I came across two books via a lecture on marketing that relate to this notion. The books show how we live in an 'attention economy', where people's attention is essentially sold and harvested. Very clever people and technology are employed to capture our attention – anticipating what our attention wants to see and hear and ensuring we are bombarded with messages about how to access this. It's fascinating to see how the attention economy came about and was manufactured, and just how pervasive and pernicious it is. Those books are by Wu, 2016 and Alter, 2018, respectively, which I mention in case you want to read them).

Too much work is not healthy: total concentration on work for prolonged periods of time is not good for us. But I spent too much time on social media or watching TV or just 'hanging around' with no real purpose in general, especially in the first year. I did so to avoid work or because of some vague idea in my head that 'work is boring', 'I can't be bothered to work now' or 'there's time for work at another point'. Even during my third year, when I was more focused and my work was improving, I'd read newsfeeds that were mind-numbing and irrelevant to me or based on sensationalism, hype and clickbait. But these feeds were able to take my time, energy and focus from me in a second. It was the same in terms of me pointlessly 'following' the portrait of other people's lives that are so carefully crafted and presented to me. In truth, I wanted distractions and the clickbait provided them. These things are designed to distract us, and they are designed by clever people and complex algorithms. We have no chance of resisting unless we are very systematic about doing so. The result was distractions from work. When the technology knows exactly what you want to see and offers it, the prospect of reading a journal article is pale!

But when time immersed in the attention economy is substituted for structured time, orientated towards working and working well (and living and living well), the results and benefits become clear. One lecturer told me in confidence that people who are focused today have the best chance in history of succeeding. He said the standards have, in some ways, never been so low. So, any individual who can focus for long enough, be disciplined and react to adversity has a real advantage as so few people can act these ways today. In a world of surface information and short-term messages, anybody who can play the long game has a clear advantage. I thought this was slightly exaggerated when I heard him say it. But when I look around, I get what he means. When I took time to listen to the stories of successful people – world-class business leaders, politicians, entrepreneurs and even sports people – I realised they were exhibiting the patience, resilience, long-term thinking and –crucially – total commitment that I think my lecturer was describing.

All I know for now is that when the phone went down and the books came up, my results improved hugely, and my thinking became crisper and less foggy. I realised that studying offers its own distractions and joys – as well as challenges. Work can be positive and affirming. I know that now. And hope I can take this attitude with me, into the next chapter of my life. 'I can't be bothered to work' should be replaced with 'great – time to work – what might

I learn here? How exciting. I can return to the easy, comfortable familiar once I complete today's aims'.

The dissertation I did is a classic case of what I'm trying to say. By the time I started my dissertation, I was more focused and aware of what good academic practice is. (Thanks, Eve, for helping explain this to me over your emails). I was also aware of how to maximise my abilities by doing certain things in my wider life. (Thanks, Titus, for your suggestions on this). But I still looked for distractions. Sometimes, I would sit and start working on my dissertation but the ping of a text message or the sound of an incoming email would capture all my attention, and I would drift and lose my train of thought. I welcomed these distractions at the start. But once I started enjoying and focusing, I didn't want them. In fact, I took the rather radical step of turning my phone off when working, becoming uncontactable and giving myself fully to the work.

Why did I do well in my dissertation (relatively) and why do I feel like the dissertation was the assessment which I enjoyed producing the most, despite it being the longest and most challenging piece of work? Perhaps, it was because I was really interested in my dissertation topic. I had agency over what I could study and how to study it. My dissertation supervisor asked me, at the start of the supervision process: 'what has interested you most on the course, what specific element of the course?' and 'what interests you outside of your degree'? These were excellent questions. I'd encourage all future students to think about these questions themselves if they are not asked similar questions by their supervisor. Answering these questions allowed me to ensure the dissertation I wrote was theoretically sound (e.g. by incorporating a particular feature of the course I enjoyed, which was negotiations, meaning I had theory and literature to draw on) but also rooted in something that interests me and which I know something about (football). Perhaps, these areas seemed incompatible. But with my supervisor's help, we were able to find a research question that was suitable for a dissertation, and which fused these areas together, thus hybridising my intellectual and life interests.

Namely, the dissertation question I focused on was: 'how important are negotiations in the football industry?' The question allowed me to unite literature and concepts in the fields of negotiations and sport, finding gaps and justification for the project. Methodologically, the process enabled me to interview some key people who have experience of negotiating in the football industry. It was fascinating to get their insights and a privilege to meet them. I enjoyed the process of framing what they said in interviews in relation to my research question. It was the first time in my life that I felt passionate about a work project. I was so proud when I handed the work in. I used to watch lecturers and wonder 'why do you care so much about this stuff?' when they were teaching. I didn't get their enthusiasm. But I genuinely think that if I were to present my findings to you now, I'd come across as strangely passionate about the data! That said, if I were advising students, I'd ensure that when they pick areas to write about, they ensure their supervisor approves their choices – the point is, the choice of subjects in response to the questions of 'what interests you' should allow an academic dissertation to evolve. It should not simply be a chance to discuss something that seems interesting, but which has no academic credibility or analytical rigour, and which therefore won't command a high grade.

I know that some students at my business school chose not to write a dissertation as their 'big' final project. It seems that other business schools give students the chance to submit alternative assessments to dissertations as their final project. At my business school, students did 'consultancy projects'. For some students – especially students who are more concerned with 'real life' business and practice – and who may find the process of writing and research especially challenging, these alternative forms of assessment may be worth looking into.

Another thing I've noticed – which seems especially pronounced now among certain students who have realised what degree classification they have got and who want a higher grade and think they deserve a higher grade – is a proclivity to enter **appeal processes**. This is where a student makes the claim that the grade they have received for a module (or number of modules) is somehow unfair and should be reconsidered. If the grade is reconsidered and they get a higher grade, in theory, their degree classification may be bolstered. Of course, by this point, the grade is almost certainly correct – it will have been graded by at least one person and **moderated**. The board of examiners will have met. The process and procedures are sound. But a student might really need a grade to be higher, so they will be willing to enter the appeal process with a sense of 'nothing to lose'. (Other students, of course, may enter the process with justification). What is the nature of the appeal? It varies and might require different things at different business schools. But the essence of the appeal is that an **assessment irregularity** has taken place. Meaning the assessment mark should be revised and appealed against.

Assessment irregularities constitute things like the lecturer having a bias or prejudice against the student or the assertion that the mark the student got does not align with the marking scheme. Needless to say, the vast majority of these claims lack substance. One course-mate I know claimed – having got a grade in the 50s – that their assessment did align with the marking scheme, and despite this alignment, he got a grade in the 50s. If this is the case, he has a point. His argument, more specifically, was that because he'd used literature in the journals the marking scheme specified, his grade was incorrect. That sounds like a good argument, in principle. In practice, however, things were more complex. While his bibliography included articles in the sorts of journals that the assessment criteria specified, the essay did not use them. The citations were just 'present' in the bibliography. They served no purpose. The citations were added in an ad hoc way, presumably in response to the marking criteria, but with no thought to analysis (or integrity). In other cases, the students used work in the journals within their essays but in a very perfunctory, even dishonest way; for example, using the citations to evidence points in the essay, despite the articles used not being directly linked to the points in question. Obviously, these inconsistencies in what the student claimed and what the reality is were easily refuted in the appeals process and the student just looked bitter.

In another case I heard about, a student claimed the lecturer had a personal problem with her, and the reason for her low grade was that the lecturer had purposefully given her a low grade when reading her work. This assertion was very hard for the student to prove. The student conceded when she learned that the module's marking was anonymous. The marker had no way of identifying her essay. With hundreds of other scripts being marked for the module, the chances of identifying the essay and then giving it a bad grade were slim, if not almost non-existent. The appeal was, frankly, fanciful to say the least and probably hurtful to the lecturer. It always amazes me that students think academics have not experienced tenuous appeals before and will somehow feel pressure to change a grade because the student has the right to enter an appeal process. The appeal process is a safety net, rather than a second chance to compensate for a lack of work in the past on the students' part.

Moving on to the here and now. In some ways, it feels like I have so many options. In other ways, it feels like my options are quite limited. I feel overwhelmed, disoriented and excited all at the same time. I once learned in a lecture about how success – especially success relating to the achievement of a long-term goal – can do strange things to one's mental state. They explained how Olympians commit so much time and energy to a goal – winning a medal. And how mountaineers also make climbing a certain mountain an ambition that takes central importance in their lives. However, once the medal is won and the mountain is climbed, there is a sense of anticlimax – a sense of 'is this all I did it for?' and – more importantly – 'but what do I do now? My entire identity was doing that, and now that has gone, who am I and what shall I do?'. The sense of purpose, structure and routine that went into achieving the goal has been taken away. There is a need to adjust and reevaluate. I am not for one second saying I feel like I have a sense of anticlimax or that acquiring a degree is comparable to winning an Olympic medal! But I do think there is a sense of 'what next?' for me – and others – and I have no clear answer to this. At school, things were always linear and routine – next year, then the next year etc. It was the same at university. What defined progress was defined for us, by those who taught us at school and business school. They mapped out our path for us. We just listened and followed. But now, the path is not clear and obvious. I have to figure out what is next. That is daunting. But there is also freedom and eclecticism about where I go from here.

Going to work and making money has its appeal. But work as what? I don't have much experience so I'm asking prospective employers to take a chance on me. I can't demand a high salary because, despite my degree, I don't have the skills and experience. I only have potential. If I had done a placement, like Titus, I would perhaps have more to offer and more to bargain with. I also don't know what I actually want to do. I feel like I want someone to come along and say 'this is what you will do, go and learn about it'. One reason I wanted to do a degree in a business school was because I thought the degree would be generic enough to keep my options open. But in some ways, it would be nice if I had more limited options; almost being forced in a certain direction.

That said, I am willing to learn and feel like I could clearly say, in an interview, why it's worth taking a chance on me. I think I can come across as someone I would employ if I was more senior and looking to hire. Also, I think that I can increase my salary over time, once I get in and show my worth, value and skills in a workplace context. I see the workplace as an extension of my degree: I have acquired skills, and I want to use these skills and I also want to learn more. Another option is to travel. The world is a big and beautiful place. A lot of students seem to want to see it and experience it. I can't blame them. But are they just running and hiding from reality? Are they just delaying the next phase of their life, in other words putting off work – or the prospect of work – delaying the next chapter of their lives? It seems like a real privilege and luxury to be able to travel. I can't afford to do that. But I don't blame anyone who can afford to travel and does.

Another option is to prolong the study experience. There are Masters degrees – at my business school and almost every business school – that look appealing and which would, on paper, make me more employable. It is very easy to enrol on these degrees, except at the most elite institutions. At the end of the day, universities make money from people studying in them! And I am sure the degrees will enhance people's skills and employability and – more importantly – be a source of enjoyment for students who are simply not ready to leave university and want to learn more. But I am done with study. I think a master's is more suited to somebody who is very academic. I know one person who is doing a master's as he plans to complete his master's and then do a PhD and become an academic. This is a lofty path and a master's is required if that path is to be walked. Their exceptional performance to date means they have fee reductions, so the master's degree is an investment: a necessary qualification on the part of a wider career path and aim. This is not the same as simply 'doing a master's because it's not clear that there is anything else, or anything better, to do. It's more debt, it's more time not earning.

There are chances to study subjects I've not done so far but which, because I'm a graduate, I'd be considered for. I can even train in law if I want! But again, for me, this does not feel like the right path. I am done with studying. Like travelling, I don't blame those who do it, and I know it's an option, but I think it's good to follow your instincts. I think if people are really honest – and block out all the noise and fear and hype – they often instinctively know what to do and, more importantly, what not to do. It's having the bravery to listen and follow one's instincts that matters, rather than swimming around with all the options in mind and overwhelming you.

So, things are up in the air. I have a graduation ceremony coming up. My family will be there. I know how proud they will be of me. In a way, the ceremony day is their day – they will get an insight into the life I've been living for the last three years, which they know so little about. They made massive sacrifices for me. Our parents generally have. Perhaps, we don't realise their sacrifices or acknowledge them enough or we realise it too late. In terms of the ceremony, it's a formal affair. We will all wear suits and I hear part of the ceremony is in Latin. I know my parents will be emotional.

I have been frantically applying for jobs. If a job comes up, I will take it. Anything! I have to be realistic. I'm not going to be an investment banker. Life is not a movie. I need to start at the bottom of some ladder. But it has to be a ladder I want to climb or a ladder that allows me to climb if I want to. Networking – who you know – is something that you both mentioned in earlier emails. I am seeing the value of networking, or 'being networked', now. I didn't make any substantive contacts as a student. I know some who did. For them, they know people or know people who know other people who can provide a 'foot in the door'. This is not the same as knowing people who are willing and able to create jobs where jobs don't exist or excluding others as part of favouritism. It is more about leveraging people you know to put you in touch with the right people who may then be able to provide a chance for you to get the right opportunities. Back home – in the old town where we all grew up – I am more networked. Or, more specifically, I have family friends who are. I suspect it is a good strategy to try and get a job through these connections. Moving home might feel like a 'step back'. Going from my university accommodation, back to my old life. However, it's not forever. It might be a step back to move two steps forward in the future. Or I might go back and end up staying, realising it is 'home', and that university was a temporary hiatus from it. I'm very fortunate, my parents don't mind me moving back! And if I do that, the home-cooked meals and other homely comforts will be very much appreciated.

That said, I feel a sense of foreboding about 'going home'. I am not the same person who I was when I left the old town. University has changed me as a person, fundamentally. When I go home to visit now, especially for longer periods of time like over the Christmas and Summer vacations, I realise how much I've changed and how much harder I find it to 'fit in' and 'have things in common' with people. I get bored by people, experiences and routines that I used to enjoy. I miss little things – like being able to get what I now call a 'proper coffee' – when I'm back. I used to think it was people in my old life who changed. Then, I realised they had stayed the same, and it was me who was different. It is me who no longer fits in there. I have different experiences and different reference points. It's interesting that when I go home now, I seem to gravitate and spend more time with people whom I didn't spend time with at school or thought I didn't like at school, but who have also gone to universities and who, therefore, I seem to have a level of solidarity and cohesion with. I guess that if these people also return 'home', I will try and involve them in my life. Perhaps, people 'back home' resent the opportunity I had. Perhaps, I give the impression I think I am better. Perhaps, they just bore me now. I noticed it acutely when I first came back for a weekend. The last day before I left to attend university as a Fresher, I went to a pub in the old town, and I saw four people I went to school with. When I went home, I went back to the pub and the same four people were in the same pub, on the same seats, talking about the same things. Maybe there's comfort and familiarity with that level of sameness. Or perhaps, it's mundane and unimaginative to a length that is unhealthy and very oppressive. In mind of this, having survived business school, I now need to survive the next stage of my life.

Thanks for all your help over the years.

To the future – whatever it may hold – let's face it with courage and kindness and optimism.

Love from
Adam

Summary of Key Points

- Students who get borderline degree classifications might have their grades boosted by the board of examiners.
- The end of studying at a business school represents the start of a new, exciting chapter. Business school should be missed and thought about with affection and nostalgia, but not mourned.

- Many options exist for the recent business school graduate – such as further study, travel and work – but what is best for a particular student at a particular point in their life is individual.
- Geography matters! Where the graduate is spatially placed upon graduation will impact the opportunities available, as a localised economy.

Things to Think About

- Where is your attention, most of the time? Are there any patterns in terms of where your attention goes and why it goes there? What commands your attention? Where should your attention be? How can you shift your attention from things that are less healthy to things that are more beneficial for you?
- How do you feel/expect to feel at the end of your degree? What state of mind should you have, as you leave business school and enter the next stage of your life?
- Are there any dangers to be aware of once you leave business school and start the next chapter of your life? How might you mitigate these dangers?
- What options do you have to pursue upon graduating from business school? What are the advantages and disadvantages of each option? How can you capitalise on any opportunities that exist?
- Are you networked? Do you have people who you can contact and ask to help you, as you move on to the next part of your life? If so, what is the best way to contact them and what is the appropriate sort of communication?
- Where will you be based, geographically, after business schools? What are the advantages and disadvantages of being spatially placed there?

Glossary of Key Terms

Appeal process: a process students have a right to engage in if they want to appeal against a grade they have received for a module.

Assessment irregularity: when a procedure or established academic convention has been violated or not properly followed as part of an assessment being formally assessed, an assessment irregularity has taken place. This may result in a particular grade being given to an assessment that the student feels is unfair. What constitutes an assessment irregularity is different at different business schools but typically includes anomalies like assignments not being graded in line with what is stipulated on the assessment brief and marking criteria or a student claiming they have been given a lower grade because those marking their work have prejudice against them.

Board of examiners: the people who meet and collectively make up 'the board' that considers students' grades – and progressions and degree classifications – at the end of the academic year. The board is usually composed of the academic teaching staff – especially module leaders – who have taught and graded the assessments that the board are meeting about. A board of examiners typically has a 'Chair', who essentially runs the board and makes final decisions, while taking board members' comments and points of view into account. The chair of the board is responsible for ensuring that procedures and processes have been appropriately and consistently followed.

Discretion: a notion that the board – especially the exam board chair – can choose to apply if they want to award a degree classification to a student who may not seem to warrant this degree classification at first glance (e.g. a student on the cusp of two grade classifications) but who, on closer expectation, may be deserving of a higher grade. If discretion is applied to a particular student for a particular reason, it is normal that all students in a similar situation will be treated with the same discretion to ensure fairness and consistency.

Exit trajectory: when a student's performance improves rapidly in their penultimate and especially final semesters, they are exiting with a 'trajectory' – that is a pattern of grades – that suggests they have made substantial progress towards the end of their degree. This may be taken into account, when the board applies discretion, to attribute a higher grade to a student.

External examiner(s): members of academic staff who teach and examine at another business school, who are invited to watch the board of examiners as they make their decisions. External examiners ensure fairness and consistency exist in the board's grade attributions and that procedures have been followed. External examiners will also evaluate, give feedback on and approve the assessments that students will be given in their modules. External examiners are sent copies of proposed assignments earlier in the year to ensure the assignments are clear and suitable for the level of study.

Moderated/moderation: the process that sees a student's piece of work marked by the module leader and then 'moderated', that is looked at by a second marker to ensure the grade given is objective and that the feedback given is suitable.

References (for job applications): when students apply for jobs, it is usual for the prospective employer to ask for a 'reference'. In some cases, a job offer is made subject to suitable references being received. A reference is written by a suitable person – such as a university lecturer or tutor, who should have a degree of familiarity with the student and their work. Through references, students, in their role as prospective employees, are described and their suitability for employment is emphasised. Their ability to learn, be on time, show respect and exhibit other positive traits may be highlighted to bolster their chance of receiving employment.

Further Reading

Wu, T (2016). The attention merchants. The epic struggle to get inside our heads. Atlantic Books.

Alter, A. (2018). Irresistible: the rise of addictive technology and the business of keeping us hooked. Penguin.

EPILOGUE

Eve's working week is a blur. It starts early and ends late. It's very expensive to live in the centre of the city where she lives. Even on her salary, she can't afford to do that unless she is willing to live in a shoebox apartment. So, for Eve, each day it's a commute – quite a long commute. She gets a train from a station, based in a part of the city that is clean and affluent, overpriced and packed with other ambitious professionals. On the train, she can do work. Thank goodness for her laptop. Nothing like getting a head start on work before she even gets to the office. Or at least that's what she used to tell herself. Some days, she distracts herself with her phone. That way she won't miss any calls that come in; she also gets to listen to those silly pop songs that she and her friends used to dance to when they were students in bars with sticky floors and cheap drinks. They were good days. She seemed to know everyone around her back then. There's not much sense of community in the area she lives now – people don't really talk to each other much. Sometimes, people raise a family in her area. But more often than not, the families move away, to more leafy suburbs. The commute is enjoyable. It was very novel to begin with. But it is starting to feel costly, in terms of time and money. But it's necessary.

By the time Eve gets home, following her day at the office and the commute back and forth, she's exhausted and it's late and she needs to get some sleep before another day arrives. Some nights she can't sleep. Her mind is going too fast, she is obsessing over details. She is worrying if she said the right, or wrong, thing. She's hyper-focused. She's seeking perfection, or perfection as the firm and its partners define it. She's not sure how to stop it. It's unhealthy. In her more honest moments, she knows she's just a resource. She's easily replaced. Her work isn't really that important. There's probably no loyalty to her. She's seen others fired and let go.

DOI: 10.4324/9781003467397-8

Weekends are spent resting and, often, catching up on work. More work at the weekend seems paradoxical. But there seems to be an inverse correlation between how much work she does during the week and how much work she 'needs' to do at the weekend. The more work she does during the week, the more – not less – needs to be done at weekends. At first, she expected it to be the other way around. She conceptualised work as a unit of time. She assumed that if she spent long enough working Monday to Friday, then units of time have been bought or earned for weekends. Respite from work. But corporate life is not like that. In her world – in the world of elite business – work creates more work. In this sense, she's a victim of her own success. If she wasn't so efficient Monday to Friday, there wouldn't be as much administrative processes and bureaucracy to satisfy at the weekends. Even though work has dominated her week, there is always something to look over, especially on Sundays. She sometimes thinks she could ease off. She's not getting paid for all this extra work. But everyone else works like this. She has to, too. She can't let others down.

At weekends, Eve doesn't go to the office. She finds a local coffee shop with Wi-Fi, and double checks all her work is in place: ordered, detailed and giving the right impression. She sometimes looks at the young baristas serving coffee. They laugh. They seem so free. Maybe it would be nice to have a job like that, instead of the one she has. She recognises people in the coffee shop who also commute during the week and who get the same trains as her, deep into the central business district, wearing well-cut suits. These people are on laptops, too, like Eve. At weekends, they are dressed less formally. Perhaps, they are also doing some 'weekend work', as Eve calls it. Perhaps, she's emailing them, and they are emailing her back, in the coffee shop as they negotiate and agree on how a deal will be ordered and structured. What an irony that would be – all those emails to someone who is sitting just over your shoulder. You can hear them typing on their laptop while sipping an expensive cappuccino, flavoured with vanilla syrup. But you communicate through emails, not face to face. The screen is the new face. Besides, an email trail is so much better if one needs to prove accountability later down the line – just ask the law team and they will tell you.

After weekend work, it's back to proper work. Eve's working life is defined by tall buildings and glass doors. Everyone is very polished. The buildings are pristine. The food in the building's restaurant borders on world class. There's even a gym that Eve can use on her lunch hour. Almost everyone in her office sounds and looks the same. Her team socialises after work on a Friday. She is establishing herself. Her name is becoming known in the firm, among those 'who matter'. She has had a number of promotions and is due another one soon. She was even headhunted by a rival firm at one point. Her current firm matched the headhunters' offer. She makes a lot of money and saves a small fraction of it. Her cost of living is high. She rarely sees her parents now. She misses them. They have visited the city a few times, but they seem overwhelmed, and Eve thinks they find her 'sort' of restaurants pretentious and overpriced.

In truth, they are intimidated by Eve's world. They love her so much. They are so proud of her. But they don't understand her world. They don't want to make a mistake and embarrass her. They don't understand the 'career girl' in front of them. She will always be their world. It's easier for Eve to visit them.

How long will Eve live like this – commuting to the city from a spacious house she rents but will probably never buy? She does not know. She loves her life. She enjoys the challenges work brings. She can't believe how lucky she's been to get this far. But is it sustainable? She needs a couple of holidays a year just to charge her batteries. She's physically and mentally exhausted. She's started to develop a hyper-anxiety – even paranoia – that she will make a mistake and that the mistake will be punished. She's even thought about seeing someone to discuss the notion of imposter syndrome. This is what they mean by 'a rat race'. But there are incentives to keep going, to keep trying to win the race. She has no plans to walk away from this. Anyway, people rely on her now – she manages a team. The team members whom she manages are mostly younger than her. They remind Eve of herself when she graduated and came to work in the City: eager to impress, ambitious and focused on becoming a partner one day. She knows some will make it, but most won't. Like so many others, they will get so far and then give up. They will find too much attrition in this life. They decide they want a slower life, and maybe a life that is more family-friendly. They move back to the towns and regional cities where they grew up.

But Eve will keep going, for now at least. Telling herself that a few more years of this will be 'enough'; that once she just delivers on the next couple of projects she can walk away, with a glittering CV and some savings, if she wants. But only if she wants. She's in control. She tells herself that all the time.

And if she was to walk away from this, what should she walk to? She's at the apex. Swap this for a boring life in a provincial town? Working with people who, in truth, would not 'make it' in her world. Besides, she seems to have lost touch with the friends she made at school and even university, except for a small few whom she knew at business school and who work for similar firms in the same part of the city and who she sometimes meets during the week, ostensibly to socialise but in reality to get information that is helpful to business decisions. Eve has made new friends since leaving business school. These friends are work colleagues. She is not sure if she trusts all of them. The point is that if Eve left this life, she'd be leaving behind not just a career but all her social contacts too. Maybe this is who she is. Maybe this is who she was destined to always be – 'the career girl', as her family call her, with a hint of envy and disparity. All the insignias of a young professional. Her CV is glittering. Prizes, projects and successes keep coming and can be used to evidence her 'strategic management', 'vision' and 'leadership'. If anything, that makes it harder to walk away. But also more important that she makes no mistakes. That she's perfect. That she embodies all the firm requires.

But among all the formal success – the things that can be measured like profit margins and client satisfaction and the quantification of strategic leadership roles – Eve's greatest success is something she isn't even aware of. It's the way others see her. Without knowing it, when she enters a room, her young team see someone they genuinely admire. They know they can trust her. To her team, Eve is a role model, in a world where so few genuine role models exist. Eve's team know she has their back and will not take advantage of their hard work and ideas. She doesn't overload them with work. She has never let them down. Rumour has it she even defended them her own boss once: he wanted to punish them for a mistake, Eve protected them. Eve naturally knows when to push individuals and how to manage individuals. She's a proper mentor. But she has no idea how grateful and appreciative her team is of her. She won't until much later in her career when they tell her – sometimes over a drink when it is perhaps packaged as drunken babble. Other times through emails and letters filled with love and appreciation. She is moved by the way others recognise her patience and kindness to them. She is seen as an example – a rare sort of leader, one who is efficient and brutally honest but somehow different to the other managers and partners. It's as if she carries a sort of light that others find so refreshing, comforting and illuminating. It's easy to be around her. People feel sad and miss her when she leaves the room, though they don't know why.

In her early years of employment – the years when she is beginning to question if this is really what she wants, the years that paranoia and drive for perfection threaten to derail her – she has no idea of the impact she has on others. Sadly, she also attracts envy and jealousy, from those less competent and from those who want the power and salary she commands. Until Eve is older, she will dwell on this envy. She will mistake undue criticism for constructive criticism because she over-trusts a few people who are more senior than her but less competent and capable than her and who disguise their nefarious intentions with polished performances and fake, superficial displays. She will obsess over negative comments and failures, ignoring all the positives. But in time she grows out of this, and she becomes wise to the tricks of others. When she does, her light grows brighter. And the city has another real commodity – a true mentor.

Eve recently saw an email from the business school she attended. She thought it was another annoying one, from the alumni department, asking graduates to donate money. But this email is different. An invitation. It's been five years since she graduated. She always meant to revisit her university city. In truth, she should go and tell the alumni office what she is doing and offer to speak to the current cohort of students as a guest lecturer. She always loved to hear guest lecturers when she was a student – people out there who have done it. But she never gets time. Besides it's so far away. The email invites her to a five-year reunion. She knows she should go. She wants to go. It would do her good. What became of the characters she studied with? She could travel up first class and stay in that swanky hotel by the river – the one she used to pass as a student, where she used to wish she could afford to stay. The one with a restaurant attached to it, where the steaks seemed so expensive. (She now realises the steaks there are cheap compared to where she eats now). She could even do some emailing on the train – tying up loose ends.

That Sunday, Eve leaves the coffee shop after doing her weekend work and buys her ticket. She books the hotel. She loves the reunion. The business school provides her with much-needed respite over a weekend of nostalgia. It won't be the last time she revisits. In a guest lecture she will give in a few years' time, a number of students from ordinary backgrounds will be inspired by Eve as she encourages them to pursue their dreams in a way they'd not heard before.

Titus graduated with a high 2:1. He worked for a year in a local consultancy firm during a 'placement year' as a student. When he graduated, he recontacted the firm. They remembered him, fondly. They invited him for an interview. It was quite informal. He had started working on a particular project when doing his placement. The project grew in the year Titus completed his final year of study. He had experience of the project and had worked with some key supervisors on it. So, it was logical and easy for Titus to return and contribute as a graduate and a full-time, permanent ongoing member of staff. He was able to make contributions quite easily. So much so that after three years he applied for a promotion, which he got. The pay improved. He has saved money. His pension is already looking healthy. Titus was thinking about buying a house. It would be a good investment, or so his parents insist. His mortgage application is approved.

But lately, Titus has developed a strange sort of feeling. He is not sure he really wants to buy a house, not in the area he lives in now, anyway. He finds that there is a lot of gossiping and materialistic thinking around him. It's starting to stifle him. His work is routine. He appreciates it. But he wonders if he could be doing more. He feels overly comfortable and overly familiar.

Unlike Eve, Titus is not in a geography where 'big players' are placed, and where distinctive sorts of opportunities are. He certainly doesn't want to live in a big city. The commute would be too much for him. And while he's capable, he's not particularly motivated by money. Work is not a big part of his life – just something that allows him to pay bills. But he has a sense of 'I can do more'. This applies to life outside of work as much as inside of work. He might go and study. He has enough saved up if he wants to fund a master's degree. In fact, he has seen some interesting master's degrees at universities abroad. Maybe a change of scene is just what he needs. Moving to a new culture – and learning a new language and meeting new people – might provide the freshness he needs. And his line manager has told him he could always come back to work at the firm, if he did want a year's hiatus. His line manager even encouraged Titus to move. 'I wish I had when I was young, you don't want to end up like me' he said. Honesty. Brutal honesty.

One area of life that has been really challenging for Titus since he graduated is the weekends. There is just so little to do; so few options to pursue during 'leisure time'. Titus was always worried about a lifestyle that he saw around him and which he knows is easy to fall into – working all week, often in a job one doesn't really like, then just waiting for the weekend to come around and spending lots at the weekend on things that are not beneficial, doing things one doesn't really like and are destructive and worse still doing these things out of a sense of boredom and a lack of imagination. Even on the weeks when Titus does all he aims during the week – eating healthily, exercising etc – he has started to drift into a routine of waiting for another aimless weekend to come around. This might suit some. Indeed, the towns and cities seem full every weekend of people doing this. Perhaps, they need the release of the weekend to escape from their problems. Perhaps, the weekend is their problem? But for Titus, right now, his instincts tell him, this path is not one to follow.

Titus is looking closely at his options and can see the sort of future he will live in if he stays on his current trajectory. He will work until retirement to pay off a mortgage. He is lucky – most people his age can't get a mortgage. He feels a sense of injustice at this. He makes more money than his friends and most in his family. He is fortunate. He should be grateful. He can 'get the drinks in' on a Saturday and not worry. He has no real responsibilities. But he's not convinced a routine, ordinary life – going to work, paying bills and retiring – is enough. Or at least enough for him now. There is a spirit of adventure inside him. But a spirit of apathy in so many others he meets and interacts this.

Titus would like to have children one day. But not yet. When he has children, he will want to ensure he has the right 'set up' for them: a house close to a good school and where other families live. But there is a period between now and that point. And he wants more. There is a small window of opportunity to make this happen. One day he wakes up and impulsively books a flight, far away. As he flies off, he feels relief. He expected to feel anxious. He doesn't. He's alone, for the first time in his life.

Titus feels guilty at first – he worries he has disappointed his parents and even the mortgage company that was going to lend him a mortgage. But in a month's time, he has no regrets. He feels alive, for the first time in years. Food tastes better, colours seem brighter. He has a sense of peace. It won't last forever. He looks in the mirror and realises he looks somehow older. But for now, he has what he seeks. And what is it that he has? He does not know. He thinks its hope or joy. It surprises him. For the first time in his life, he trusts that he can let go and not have to try and control everything and that he has nobody to answer to or justify his decisions to. It's as if he is wearing a pair of shoes that give him freedom. He manages to retain this feeling – or something close to it – for the rest of his life. Even when he gets older and life's anxieties and challenges come at him. He has trust that 'the dots will join'. He remembers an old recording that a crazy eccentric lecturer showed him at university. It was a recording of the late Steve Jobs, talking about the importance of trusting. He now thinks he knows what Jobs meant and why the lecturer showed it.

Adam's life unfolds in line with the model of 'the late bloomer'. At university, a slow start was followed by slow progress, eventually culminating in graduation and a 2:1. Post-university saw a similar story: a slow start, leading to progress. In his case, huge progress, at least in terms of the acquisition of economic capital and later, more importantly, in terms of philanthropy, charity and goodwill.

After leaving university, Adam couldn't get work for a while. He moved back in with his parents. He sent a large amount of job applications out to a large number of places. Perhaps, after the first few rejections, he lost enthusiasm and stopped working as hard as he might to find a job. He was poor economically, but his life was comfortable – maybe too comfortable – in his parents' house. He started questioning if getting a job was worth the hassle. Besides, all the people he knew who worked seemed to hate working. For a while, Adam started spending time with other bored, largely unemployed people he knew. A sense of apathy united them; a feeling that 'we deserve better' and it's the fault of politics, society or other generations or other people that life is not how we want. They listened to music and people who affirmed this position. But Adam had the sense to realise this ideology was wrong and not right to follow. His choice of friends had to change. The same traps that snared him in his first year of university were all around him now. But unlike in his first year, this time – post-graduation – Adam recognised them. In this sense, university was all worth it. A most valuable lesson, namely knowing the importance of keeping good company, had been learned and was now acted on.

Then, one day, out of the blue, Adam has a business idea. He is sick of claiming benefits. He registers as a sole trader. The idea seems almost laughable to him: he spots a need in the local market that is so obvious that it seems unlikely to work. Why would no one else do this? Is this a case of introducing the right business in the right place at the right time? The essence of what some of his lecturers emphasised to him. To begin with, Adam makes little money. Some months he loses money. But he believes in the idea. He believes in himself. And he works and works and works. And he reminds himself he has nothing to lose anyway. He is not risking a house or a job on the idea. He has nobody to support. This is not a gamble. This is the ideal time in his life to start a business and pursue it. And one day Adam realises he has something resembling a profitable business with a product that is in demand. For a while, Adam has been selling locally. But within a year, he is selling nationally. Within two years, he is selling internationally. He starts to hire other people. He sells more units. He employs more people to help service the demand. He forms another three companies. He is amazed at how much easier business start-up feels now.

Business has become something he can do on instinct. One company fails. He doesn't care. Two are huge successes. He wakes up one day and he realises he is an entrepreneur. Another day he realises he can afford to pay himself a million pounds. These are significant milestones.

One Sunday, he goes for lunch at his parents' house. He visits the little room he grew up in. The same little room he started that first business in. He can't believe how far he has come. While there, he sees an email he sent while he was a student to Eve. He wonders what happened to her. She always had a spirit or energy or vibe he liked without knowing why. He trusted her. He reads the email. Three sentences catch his attention:

> 'Currently I want to form my own business when I leave university and employ lots of people and grow a 'proper' business like the ones we've been learning about in the early lectures. This might seem like a lofty ambition and it's one I did not have before enrolling here. Maybe in time I will realise this dream'.

He'd forgotten he wrote this. He forgot his younger self had this 'dream'. But it came true. Perhaps, it was the power of his subconscious. What we tell ourselves is so important. We are self-affirming and self-fulfilling beings. He believes that with all his heart. It's why he keeps his thoughts as positive, clean and honest as he can these days.

Later in life, Adam learns the value of money. He becomes very rich. He sells companies and forms new ones. The press labels him as 'the man with the Midas touch'. At one point, he realises he has enough money. (In fact, he realises he had enough many years ago). He does something refreshing. He doesn't get greedy. He doesn't want more. In fact, he wants to give. He wants to sacrifice. He becomes philanthropic. It's not easy for him to do this, despite his wealth. Society tells him to 'store' and hoard his money or invest it. More, more and more. The phrase 'greed is good' springs to mind the first time he donates a large amount to charity. But he resists. The power of money is in the good it can do. He is selective about who he gives money to and why. He doesn't want to give money away just for others to squander it. He wants to exercise control over what the money is spent on. A large amount of his wealth goes to help children. Children who need it. Children whose lives would suffer or be ended prematurely without it. Doing this made the whole journey worthwhile. He gets more pleasure from helping others. He's always been a selfish being by nature. He can't believe it.

Eve sits in a well-lit, polished café in a leafy suburb one Sunday, checking over the details of a mergers and acquisition proposal which will see her employer buy another company and essentially monopolise the market. The same Sunday, Titus sits in bed, at peace, thinking of nothing in particular but how great it is to be in good health and looking forward to his breakfast.

Neither Titus nor Eve have any idea that the emails they sent to Adam back when Adam was a disorganised business school student would have the impact they did. But their emails impacted Adam fundamentally.

Occasionally, Titus and Eve read about Adam in the pages of the business sections of the newspapers they peruse. ('Hey, I used to know him, that man with the Midas touch, I played rugby with him'. Titus once told his children when they mentioned a new app designed by the technological wing of Adam's company). Titus and Adam's emails impacted countless others, those Adam's philanthropy benefited. Though Titus and Adam have no idea of this. They can't see their part in a complex web of actions, results and influence. If Adam had not passed his degree – if Adam had dropped out in the first year and not had Eve and Titus to direct him – would his future, and the futures of others, have been different?

That's a question for a philosophy department, not a business school student.

Glossary of Key Terms

Central business district: the physical area of a city, where 'business is done', and therefore where the predominant companies, physical business capital and human capital are based.

Headhunted: where a person working for one organisation is approached by another organisation and offered another job, or 'poached'. Normally, with improved financial incentives.

Imposter syndrome: the psychological state of mind that arises when an individual doubts their ability to do a job and feels incompetent in comparison with those around them.

'The Man with the Midas touch': the notion that everything one does makes money and is financially successful.

INDEX

For Product Safety Concerns and Information please contact our EU
representative GPSR@taylorandfrancis.com
Taylor & Francis Verlag GmbH, Kaufingerstraße 24, 80331 München, Germany

www.ingramcontent.com/pod-product-compliance
Lightning Source LLC
Chambersburg PA
CBHW061257220326
41599CB00028B/5690